For Engineers & Designers

RHINOCEROS 3D EXERCISES

200 3D PRACTICE DRAWINGS

SACHIDANAND JHA

Dear Reader,

Thank you for choosing **RHINOCEROS 3D EXERCISES** book. This book is part of a family of premium-quality CADIN360 books, all of which are written by Outstanding author who combine practical experience with a gift for teaching.

CADIN360 was founded in 2016. More than 3 years later, we're still committed to producing consistently exceptional books. With each of our titles, we're working hard to set a new standard for the industry. From the paper we print on, to the authors we work with, our goal is to bring you the best books available.

I hope you see all that reflected in these pages. I'd be very interested to hear your comments and get your feedback on how we're doing. Feel free to let me know what you think about this or any other CADIN360 book by sending me an email at contactus@cadin360.com.

If you think you've found a technical error in this book, please visit
https://cadin360.com/contact-us/.
Customer feedback is critical to our efforts at CADIN360.

Best regards,

Sachidanand Jha
Founder & CEO, CADIN360

RHINOCEROS 3D EXERCISES

Published by
CADIN360
cadin360.com

Limit of Liability/Disclaimer of Warranty:

Examination Copies

Electronic Files

Disclaimer:

Preface

RHINOCEROS 3D EXERCISES

❖ This book contain 200 CAD practice exercises and drawings.

❖ This book does not provide step by step tutorial to design 3D models.

❖ S.I Unit is used.

❖ Predominantly used Third Angle Projection.

❖ This book is for **RHINOCEROS 3D** and Other Feature-Based Modeling Software such as Inventor, Catia, SolidWorks, NX, Solid Edge, AutoCAD, PTC Creo etc.

❖ It is intended to provide Drafters, Designers and Engineers with enough 3D CAD exercises for practice on **RHINOCEROS 3D**.

❖ It includes almost all types of exercises that are necessary to provide, clear, concise and systematic information required on industrial machine part drawings.

❖ Third Angle Projection is intentionally used to familiarize Drafters, Designers and Engineers in Third Angle Projection to meet the expectation of world wide Engineering drawing print.

❖ Clear and well drafted drawing help easy understanding of the design.

❖ This book is for Beginner, Intermediate and Advance CAD users.

❖ These exercises are from Basics to Advance level.

❖ Each exercises can be assigned and designed separately.

❖ No Exercise is a prerequisite for another. All dimensions are in mm.

❖ Note: Assume any missing dimensions.

EX-01

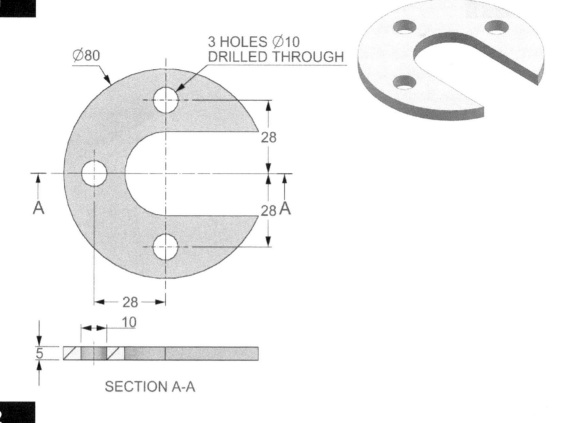

Ø80

3 HOLES Ø10
DRILLED THROUGH

28

28 A

A

28

10

5

SECTION A-A

EX-02

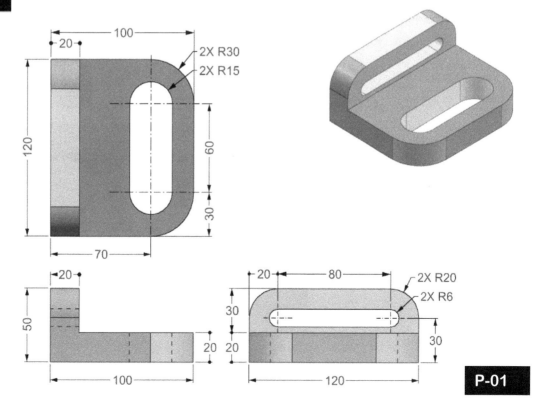

100

20

2X R30

2X R15

120

60

30

70

20

50

20

20

100

20

80

2X R20

2X R6

30

30

120

P-01

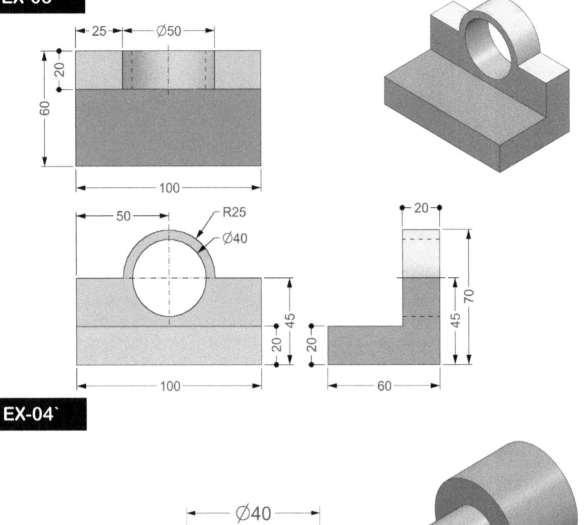

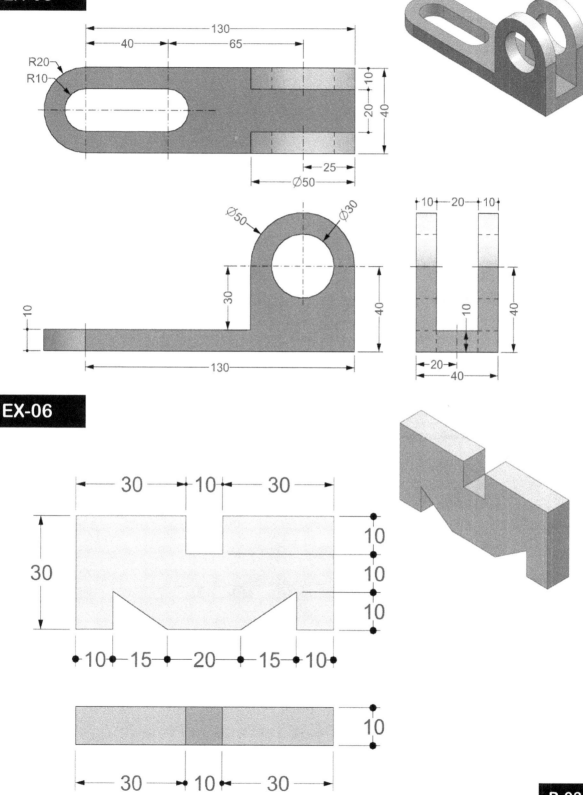

EX-05

EX-06

P-03

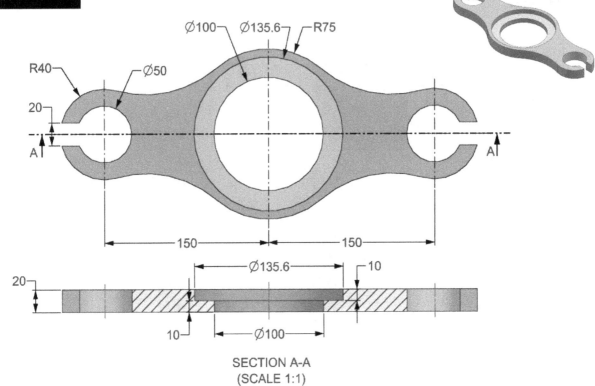

Ø100 Ø135.6 R75

R40 Ø50

20

A

A

150 150

Ø135.6 10

20

10 Ø100

SECTION A-A
(SCALE 1:1)

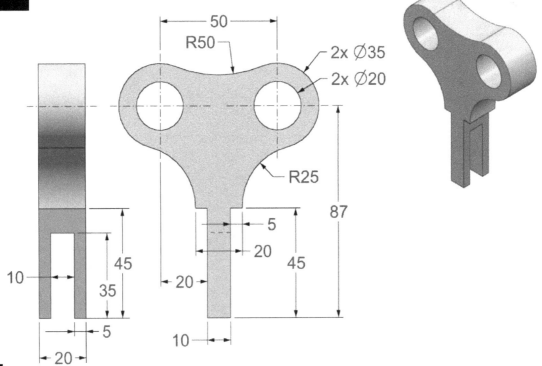

50

R50

2x Ø35

2x Ø20

R25

87

5

20

45

10 45

20

10 35

5

20

EX-09

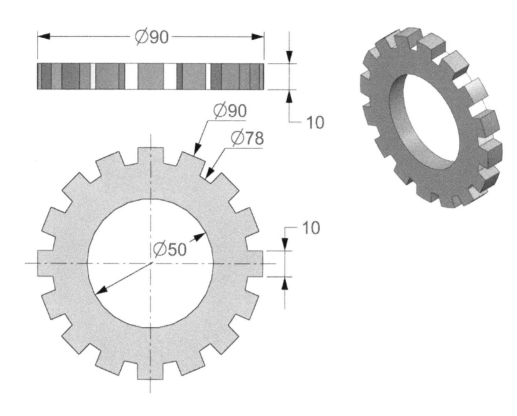

Ø90

10

Ø90
Ø78
Ø50
10

EX-10

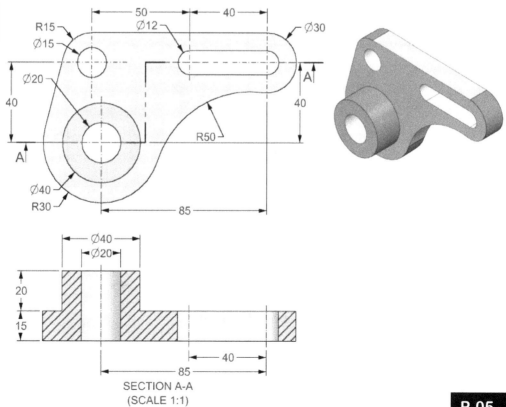

R15
Ø15
Ø20
40
Ø40
R30

50
40
Ø12
Ø30
A
40
R50
85
A

Ø40
Ø20
20
15
40
85
SECTION A-A
(SCALE 1:1)

P-05

EX-11

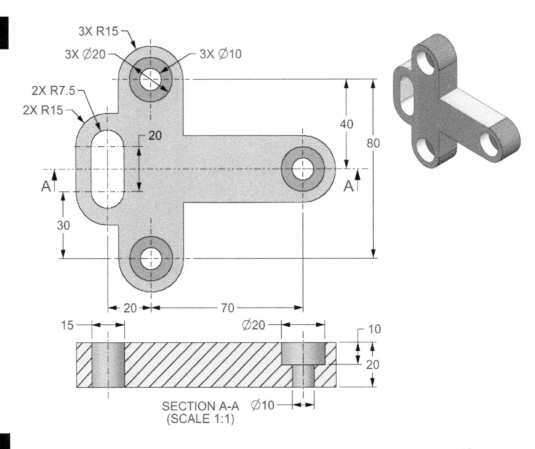

3X R15
3X Ø20
3X Ø10
2X R7.5
2X R15
20
40
80
A
A
30
20
70

15
Ø20
10
20

SECTION A-A
(SCALE 1:1)
Ø10

EX-12

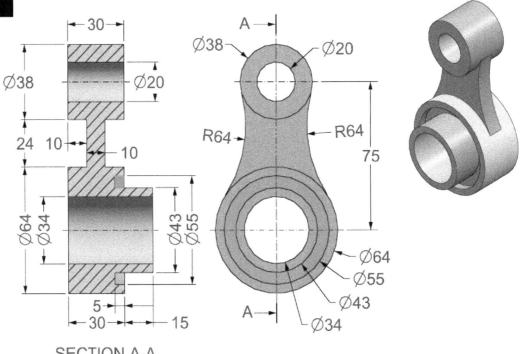

30
Ø38
Ø20
24 10
10
Ø64 Ø34
Ø43 Ø55
5
30
15

A
Ø38
Ø20
R64
R64
75
Ø64
Ø55
Ø43
Ø34
A

SECTION A-A
(SCALE 1:1)

P-06

EX-13

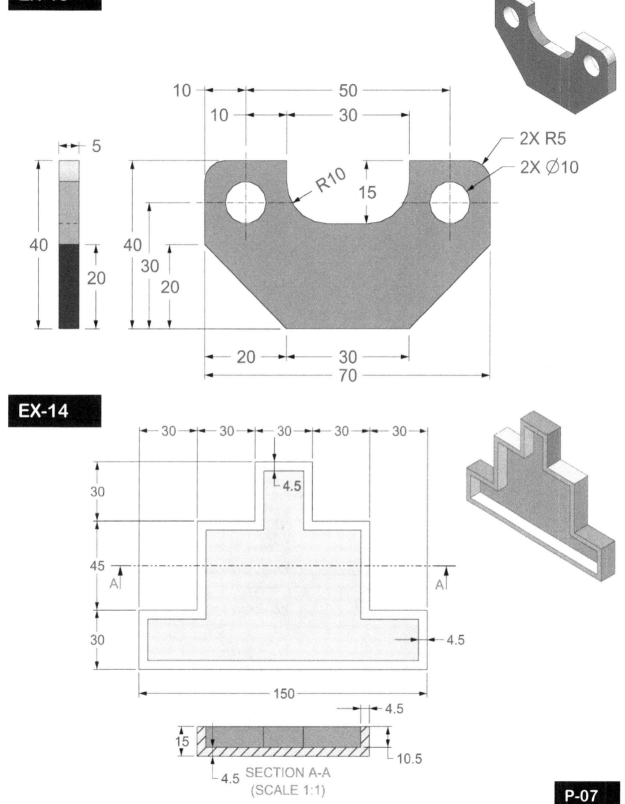

10

50

10

30

2X R5

2X Ø10

R10

15

5

40

20

40

30

20

20

30

70

EX-14

30 30 30 30 30

30

4.5

45

A

A

30

4.5

150

4.5

15

10.5

4.5 SECTION A-A
(SCALE 1:1)

P-07

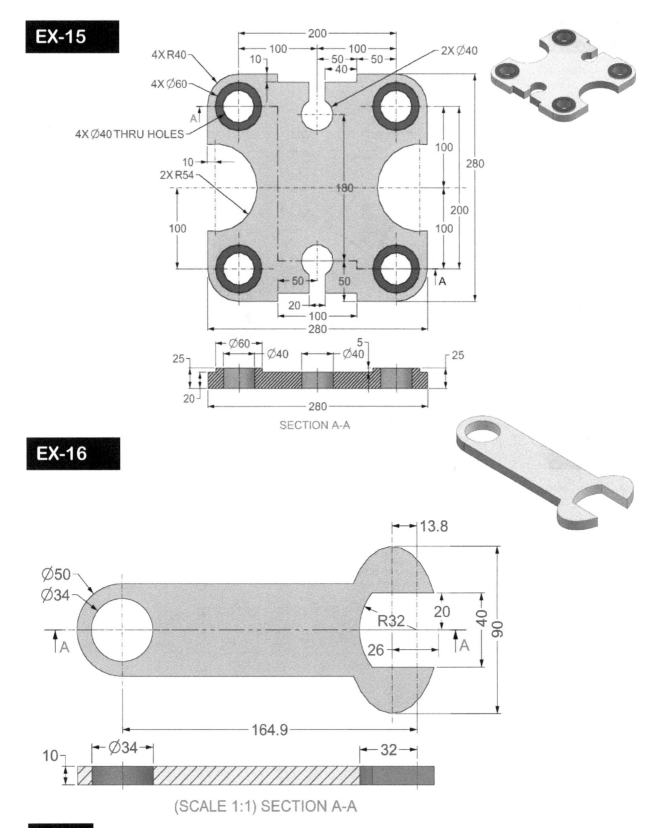

EX-15

4X R40
4X Ø60
4X Ø40 THRU HOLES
2X R54
2X Ø40

200
100
100
10
50
50
40
100
280
180
200
100
100
10
100
50
50
20
100
280

A

SECTION A-A

Ø60
Ø40
5
Ø40
25
25
20
280

EX-16

Ø50
Ø34
13.8
R32
20
40
90
26
164.9

10
Ø34
32

(SCALE 1:1) SECTION A-A

P-08

EX-17

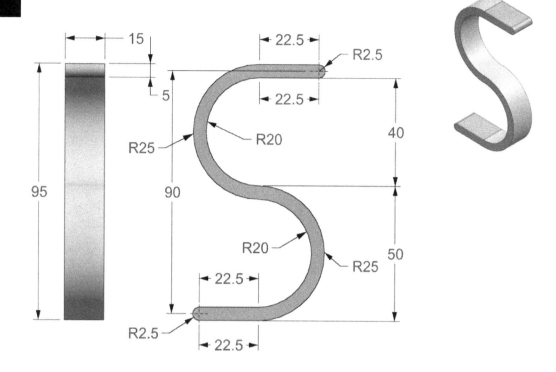

15

22.5

R2.5

5

22.5

R25

R20

40

95

90

R20

50

R25

22.5

R2.5

22.5

EX-18

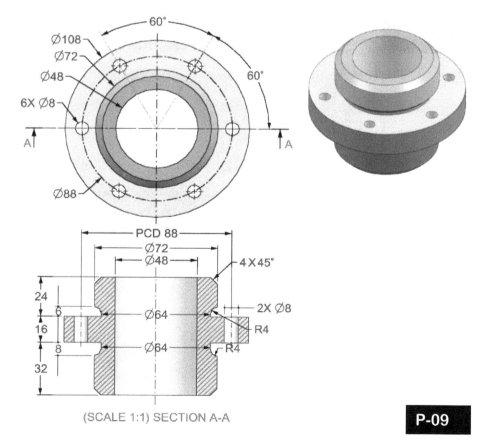

60°

Ø108
Ø72
Ø48

6X Ø8

60°

A

A

Ø88

PCD 88
Ø72
Ø48

4 X 45°

24
6

Ø64

2X Ø8

16

R4

8

Ø64

R4

32

(SCALE 1:1) SECTION A-A

EX-19

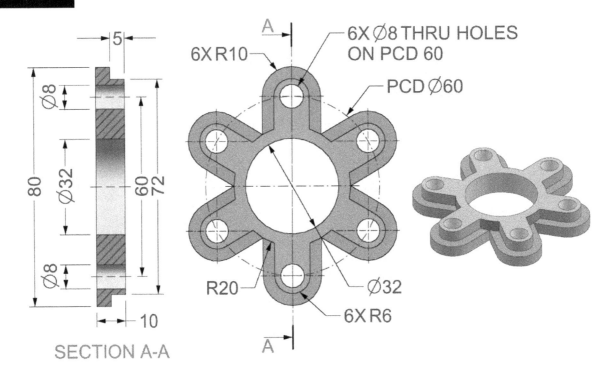

6X R10

6X Ø8 THRU HOLES
ON PCD 60

PCD Ø60

Ø8
Ø32
80
Ø32
60
72
Ø8
5
10

R20

Ø32

6X R6

SECTION A-A

EX-20

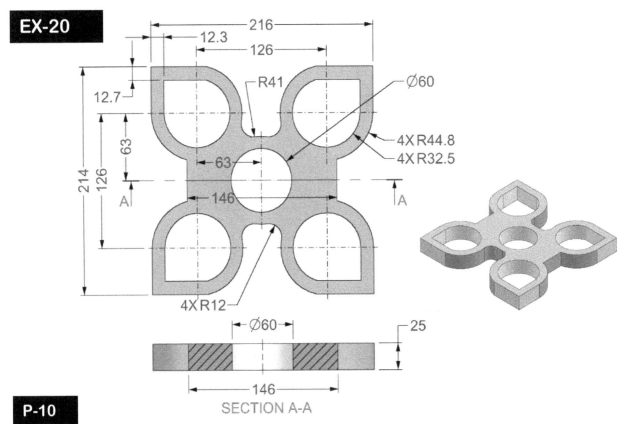

216
12.3
126
12.7
R41
Ø60
63
63
4X R44.8
4X R32.5
214
126
A
146
A
4X R12

Ø60
25
146
SECTION A-A

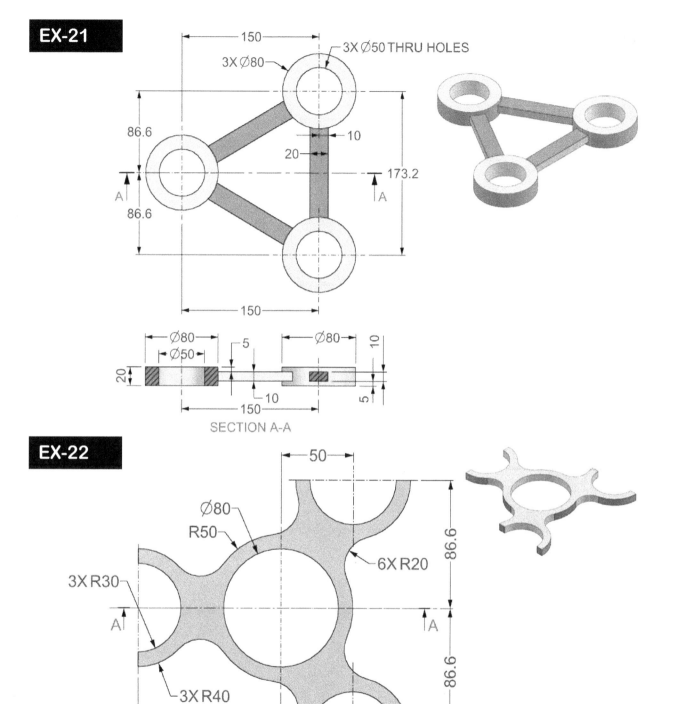

EX-21

150
3X Ø80
3X Ø50 THRU HOLES
86.6
10
20
173.2
A
A
86.6
150

SECTION A-A

Ø80
Ø50
5
Ø80
10
20
10
5
150

EX-22

50
Ø80
R50
86.6
6X R20
3X R30
A
A
3X R40
86.6
100
50

SECTION A-A

10
Ø80

P-11

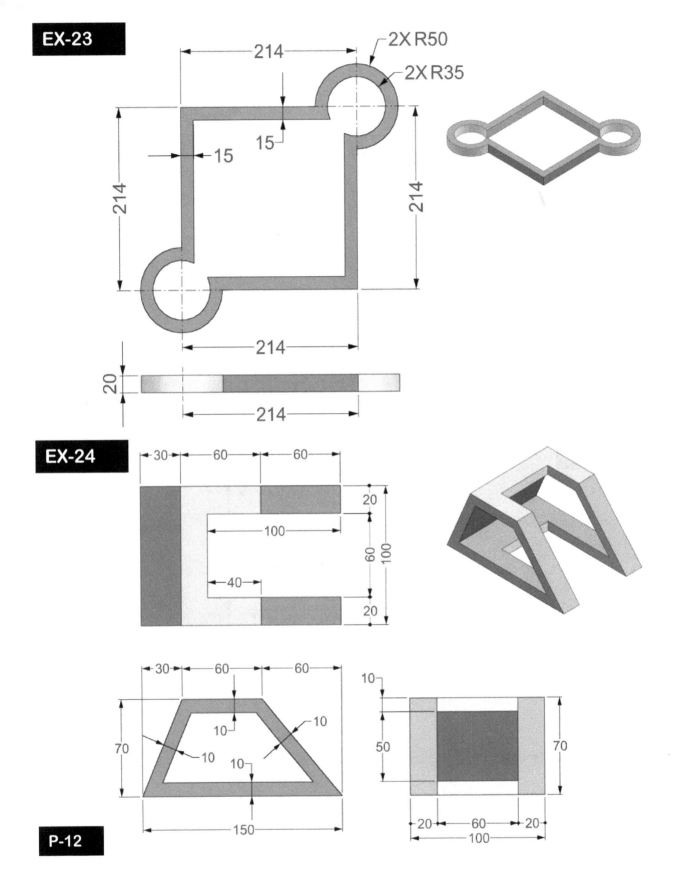

EX-23

2X R50
2X R35
214
15
15
214
214
214
20
214

EX-24

30
60
60
20
100
60
100
40
20

P-12

30
60
60
10
10
10
10
10
10
70
150

10
50
70
20
60
20
100

EX-25

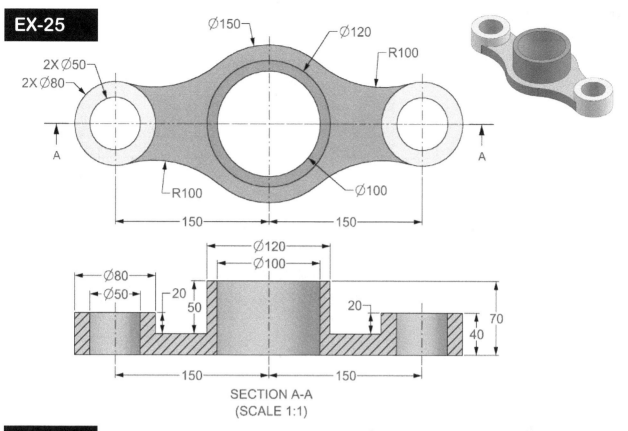

Ø150
Ø120
R100
2X Ø50
2X Ø80
R100
Ø100
150
150

Ø120
Ø100
Ø80
Ø50
20
50
20
70
40
150
150

SECTION A-A
(SCALE 1:1)

EX-26

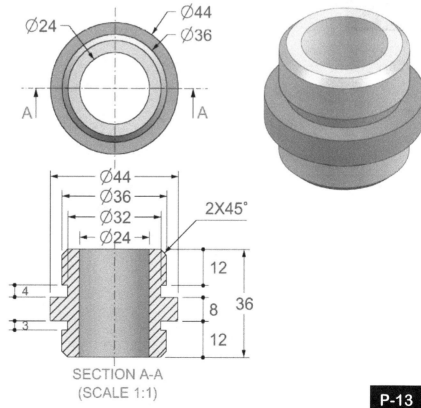

Ø24
Ø44
Ø36

A   A

Ø44
Ø36
Ø32
Ø24
2X45°
12
4
8
36
3
12

SECTION A-A
(SCALE 1:1)

EX-27

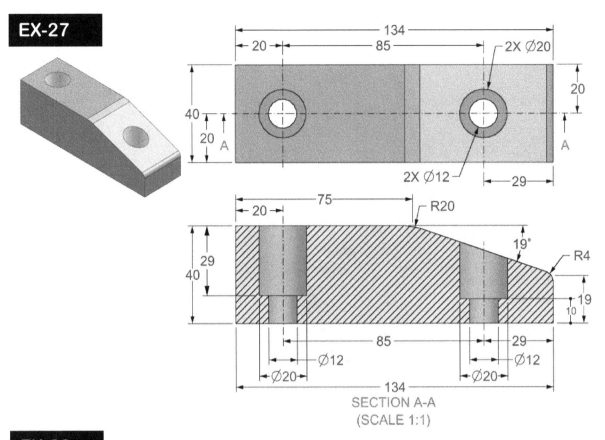

134
20
85
2X Ø20
40
20
20
A
20
A
2X Ø12
29

75
R20
20
19°
R4
29
40
19
10
85
29
Ø12
Ø12
Ø20
Ø20
134

SECTION A-A
(SCALE 1:1)

EX-28

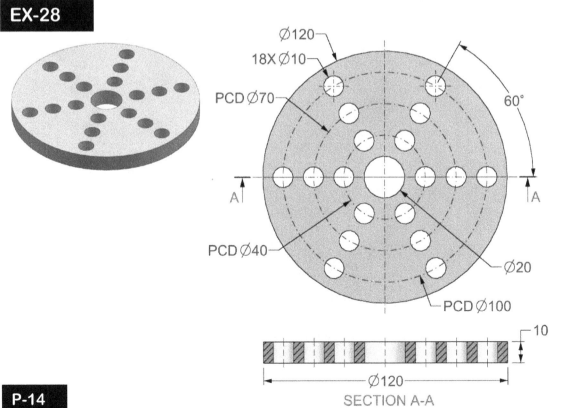

Ø120
18X Ø10
PCD Ø70
60°
PCD Ø40
Ø20
PCD Ø100

10
Ø120
SECTION A-A

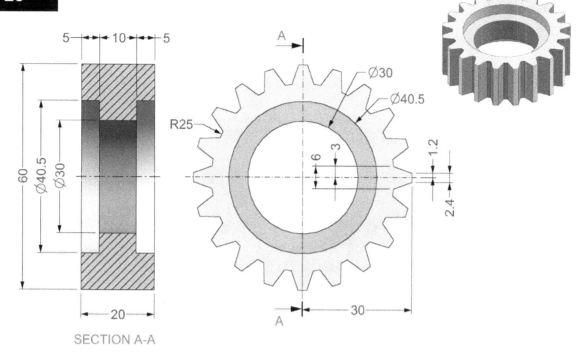

SECTION A-A

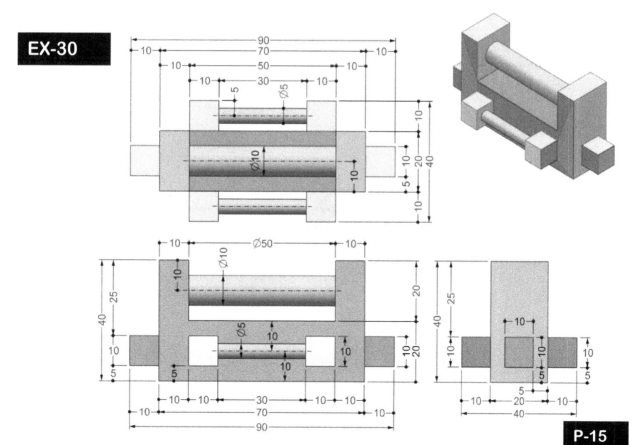

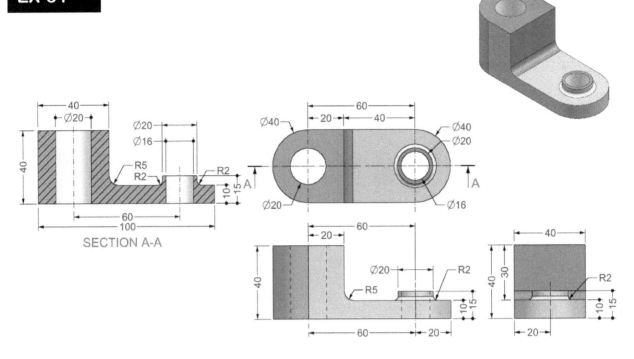

SECTION A-A

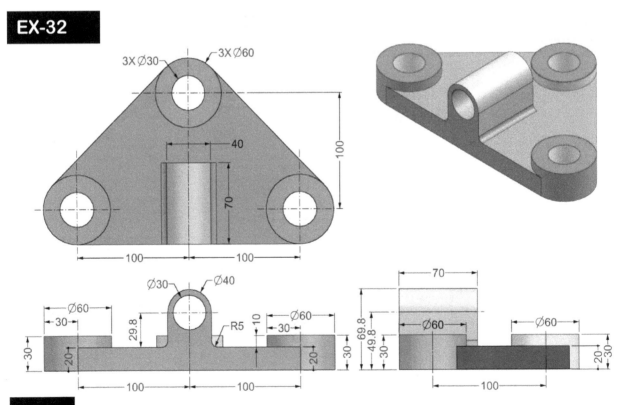

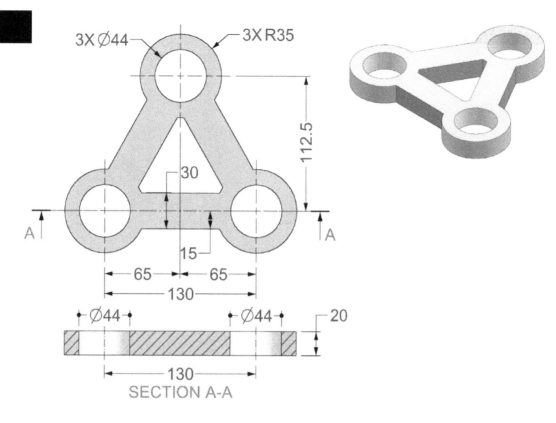

3X Ø44   3X R35

112.5

30

A   A

15

65   65

130

Ø44   Ø44   20

130

SECTION A-A

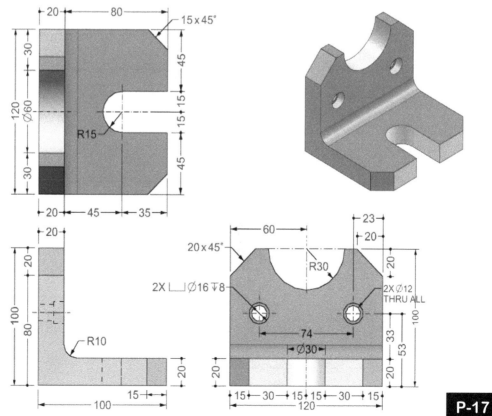

20   80   15 x 45°

30

45

120   Ø60   15 15

R15   15

30   45

20   45   35

20

20

100   80

R10

20

15

100

60   23   20

20 x 45°   R30   20

2X ⌴ Ø16 ⤓8   2X Ø12 THRU ALL

74   100

Ø30   33   53

20   20

15   30   15   15   30   15
120

EX-35

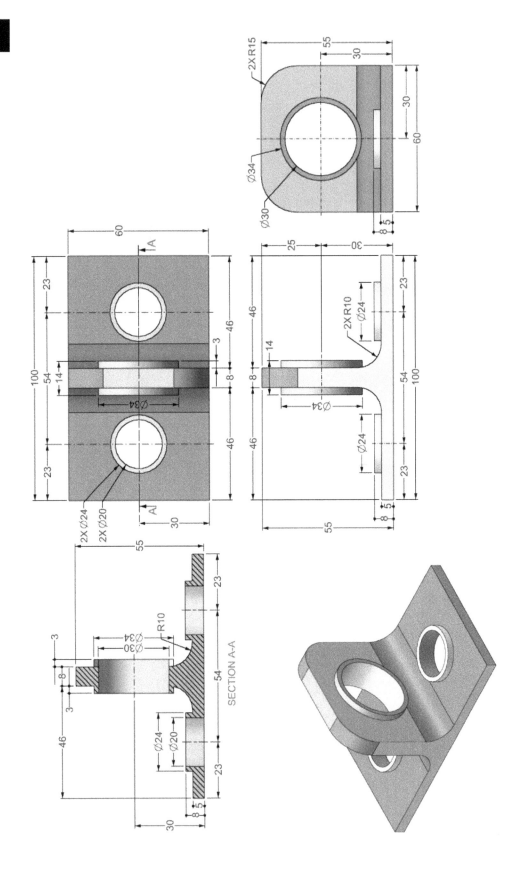

2X R15

55

30

30

60

Ø34

Ø30

8
5

60

A

23

46

3

Ø34

14

54

100

23

46

30

2X Ø24

2X Ø20

A

25

30

46

2X R10

Ø24

14

8

23

54

100

Ø34

Ø24

46

23

8
5

55

55

23

R10

3

Ø34

Ø30

8

54

3

Ø24

Ø20

46

8
5

23

30

SECTION A-A

P-18

EX-36

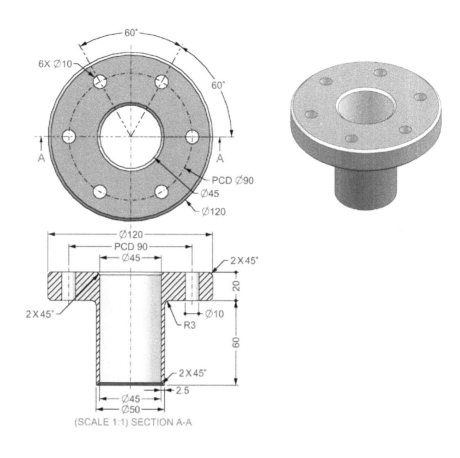

60°

6X Ø10

60°

PCD Ø90
Ø45
Ø120

A   A

Ø120
PCD 90
Ø45
2 X 45°
20
2 X 45°
Ø10
R3
60
2 X 45°
2.5
Ø45
Ø50

(SCALE 1:1) SECTION A-A

EX-37

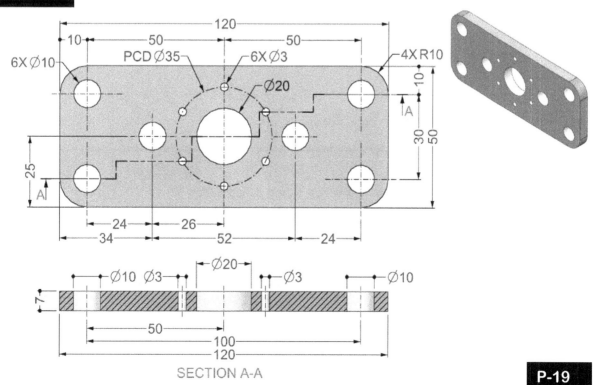

120
10   50   50
6X Ø10   PCD Ø35   6X Ø3   4X R10
Ø20
10
A
30   50
25
A
24   26
34   52   24

Ø20
Ø10   Ø3   Ø3   Ø10
7
50
100
120
SECTION A-A

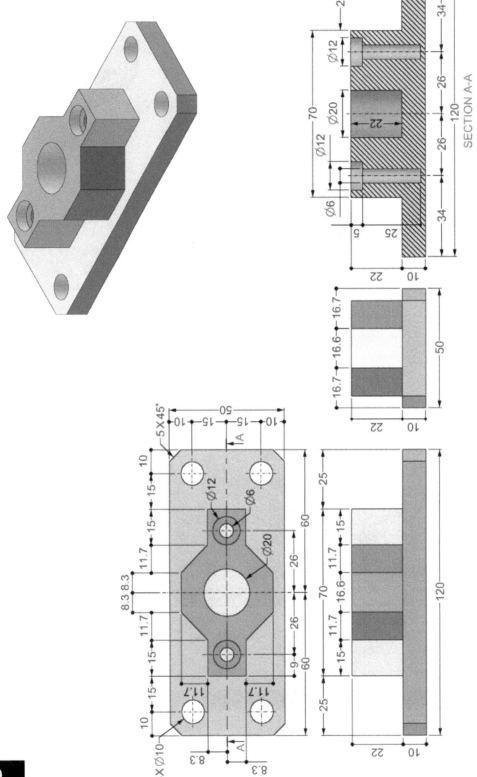

SECTION A-A

EX-39

70

R20
Ø20

40

45

45

R25
Ø20

20

30

10

10

A

A

45

65

20

2X R10

Ø40

Ø20

25

45

SECTION A-A

EX-40

Ø60

20

10

5

Ø50

Ø60

Ø50

5 — 10 — 5

30

Ø60

20

P-21

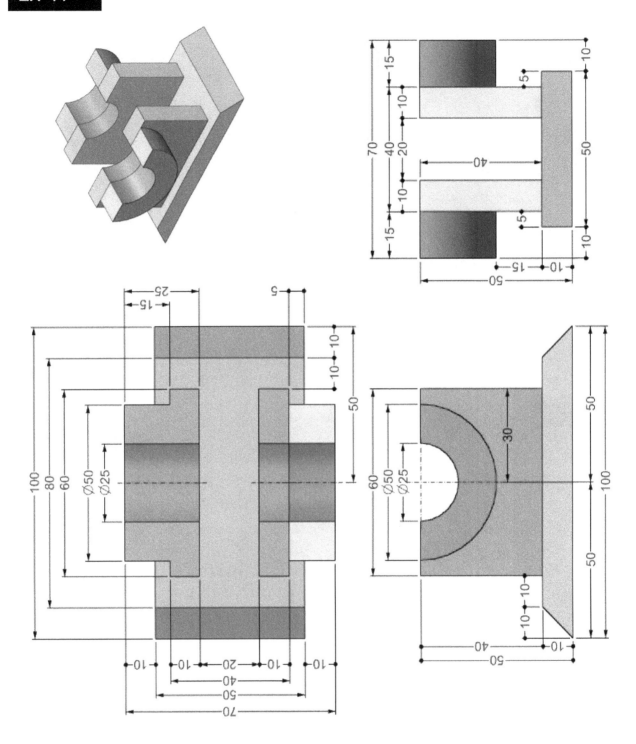

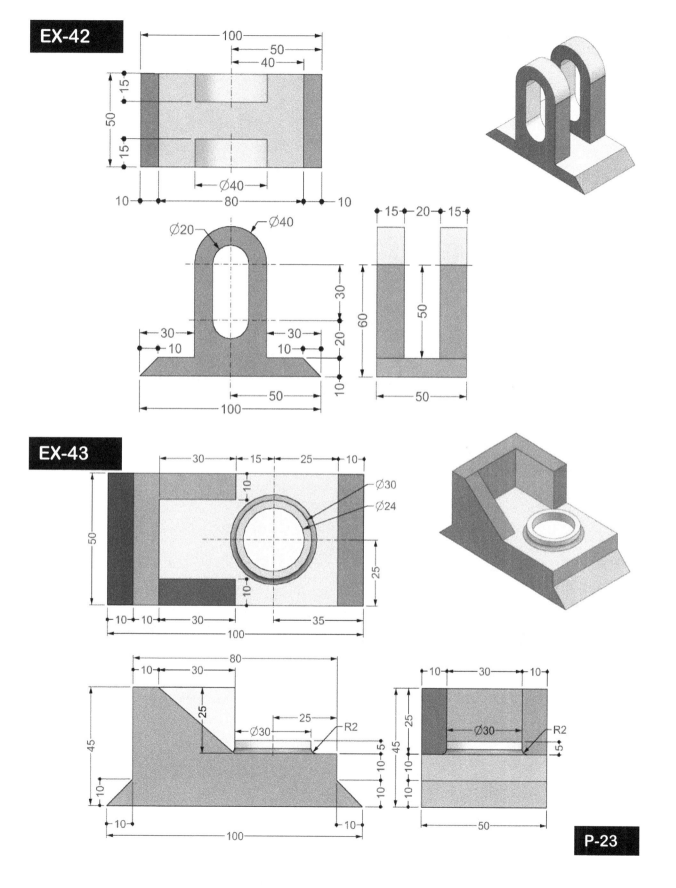

EX-42

EX-43

P-23

EX-44

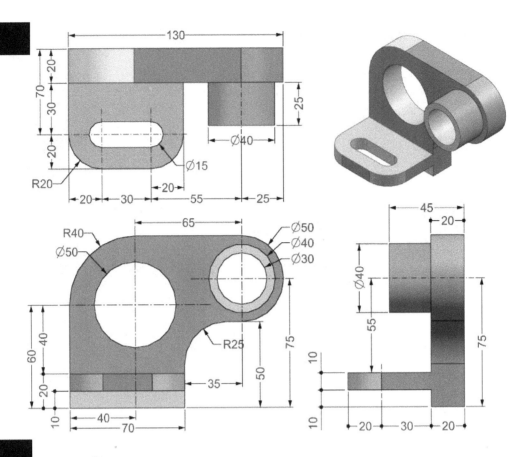

EX-45

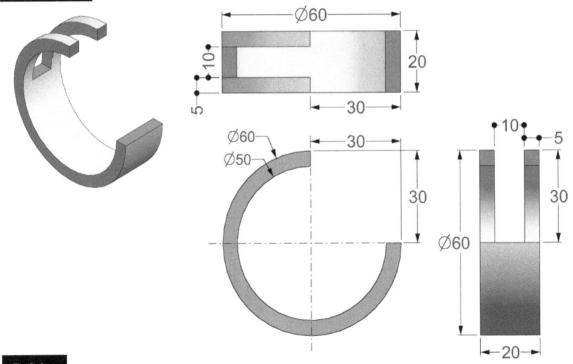

EX-46

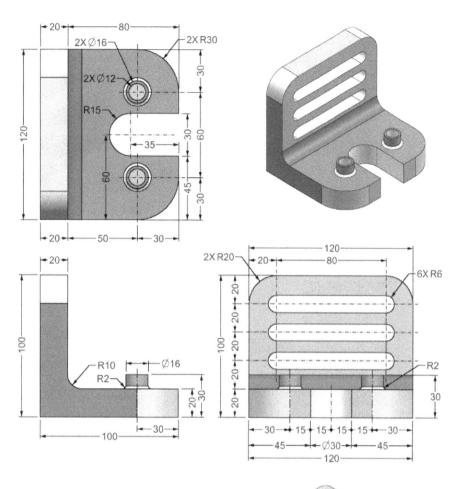

EX-47

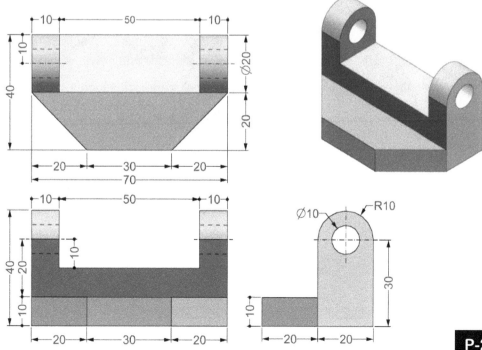

EX-48

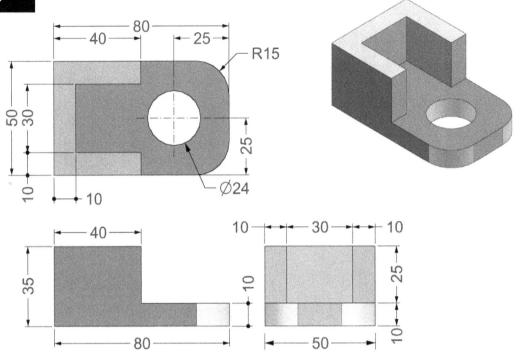

80
40
25
R15
50
30
25
Ø24
10
10

40
35
80

10
30
10
10
25
50
10

EX-49

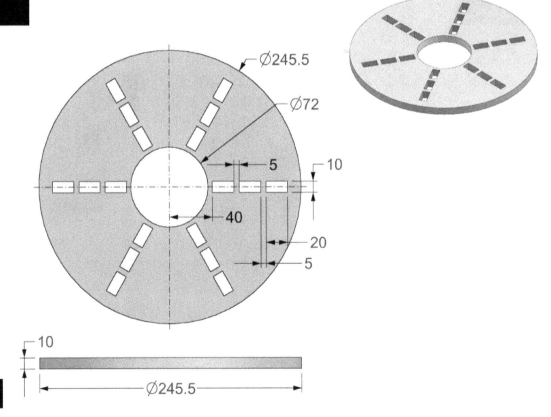

Ø245.5
Ø72
5
10
40
20
5

10
Ø245.5

P-26

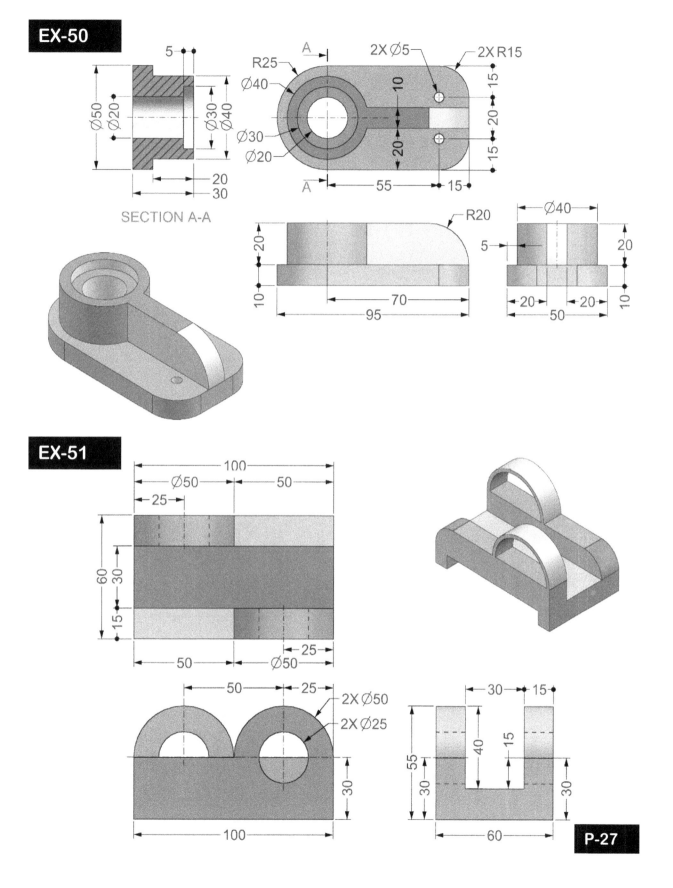

EX-50

5
Ø50
Ø20
20
30

R25
Ø40
Ø30
Ø20
2X Ø5
2X R15
10
20
15
20
15
55
15

A

SECTION A-A

R20
20
10
70
95

Ø40
5
20
20
50
20
10

EX-51

100
Ø50
50
25
60
30
15
50
Ø50
25

50
25
2X Ø50
2X Ø25
30
100

30
15
55
30
40
15
30
60

P-27

EX-52

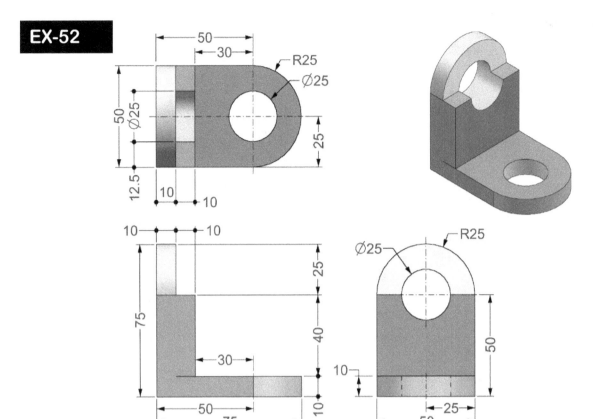

EX-53

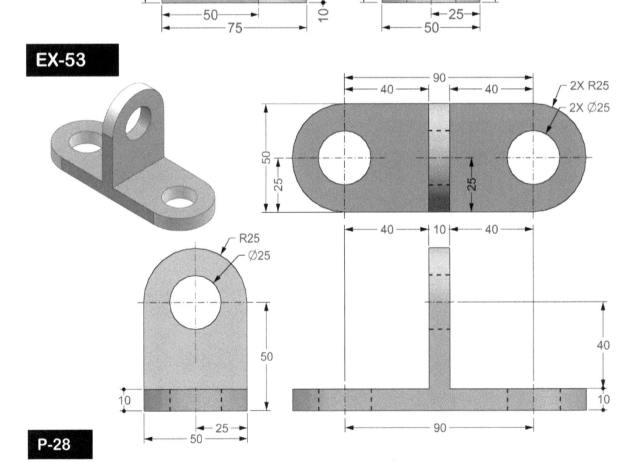

EX-54

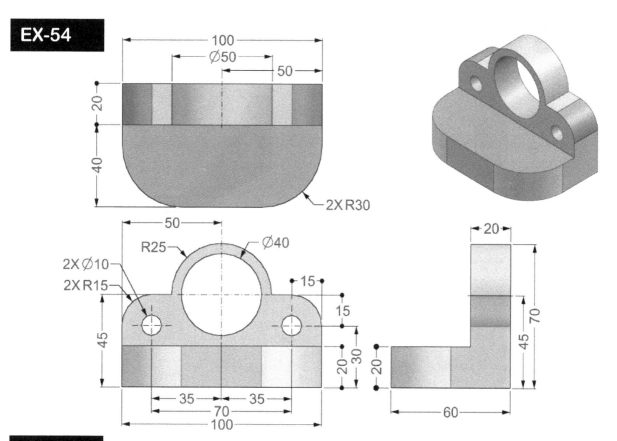

- 100
- Ø50
- 50
- 20
- 40
- 2X R30
- 50
- R25
- Ø40
- 2X Ø10
- 2X R15
- 15
- 15
- 45
- 20
- 30
- 35
- 35
- 70
- 100
- 20
- 70
- 45
- 20
- 60

EX-55

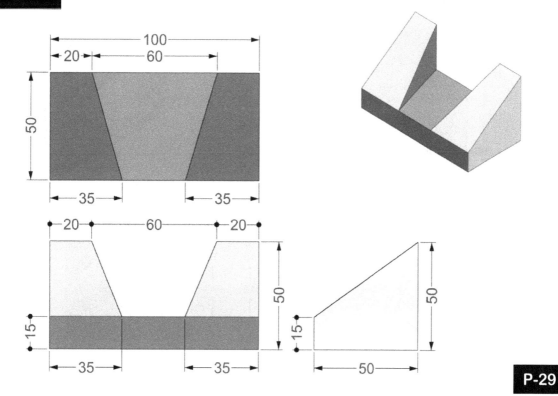

- 100
- 20
- 60
- 50
- 35
- 35
- 20
- 60
- 20
- 50
- 15
- 35
- 35
- 15
- 50
- 50

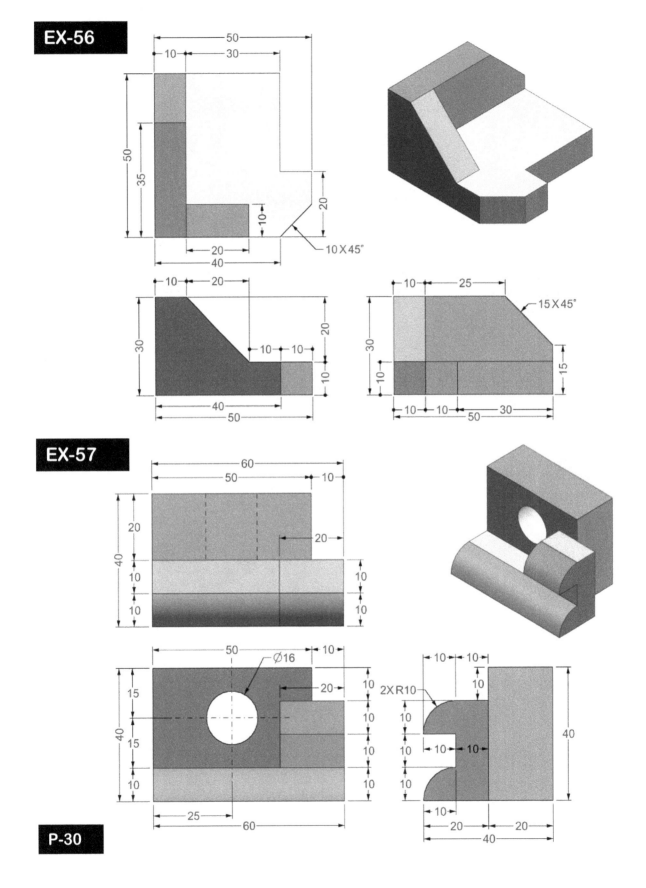

EX-56

EX-57

P-30

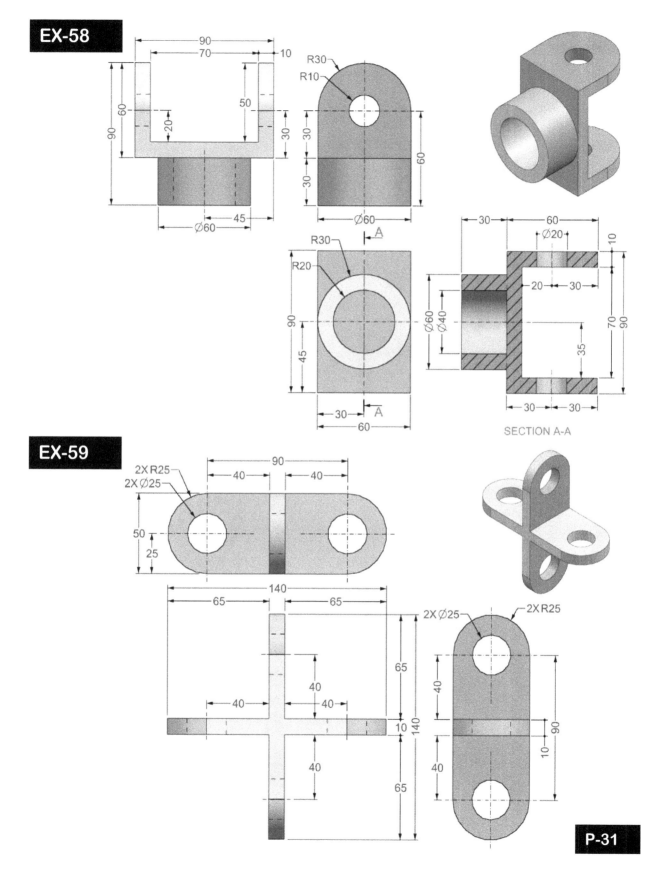

EX-58

R30
R10

90
60
70
10
50
20
30

Ø60
45
Ø60

R30
R20

90
45

30
60

A

30
60
Ø20
10

20
30

Ø60
Ø40

70
90

35

30
30

SECTION A-A

EX-59

2X R25
2X Ø25

90
40
40

50
25

140
65
65

65

40
40
40

10

40

65

2X Ø25
2X R25

40

90

10

40

P-31

EX-60

Ø50   2X Ø10   22.5
15
25
60
43.9
10
15
25
50   45
95

Ø50
Ø40
R4   R10
10
R10
40
155
130
10
45   45
80
140
R10   R10
55
30   40
10   10
22.5   22.5
100

60
85.4
100
155
34.6
10   25
40
60

EX-61

Ø120
20
R3
50
Ø50
R2
10 10 10
Ø50
Ø70

14 14
PCD Ø90   R60
Ø70   Ø30
Ø50   6X Ø10
66
132
14
14
A   A
66
66   66
132

132
Ø70
Ø50
Ø30
Ø10
10 10 10
R2
Ø50
Ø80
50   100
R3
Ø10
45   45
90
20
Ø120
SECTION A-A

Ø120   6X Ø10
PCD Ø90   ON PCD 90
Ø30
66
132
14
14
14   14
66   66
132

P-32

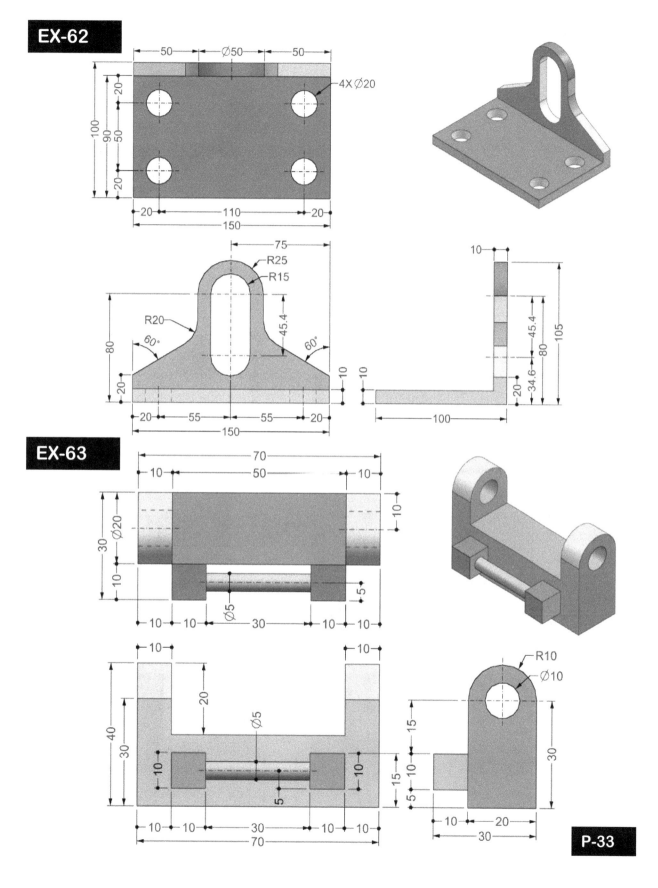

EX-62

4X Ø20

Ø50

R25
R15
R20
60°
60°

EX-63

Ø20

Ø5

Ø5

R10
Ø10

P-33

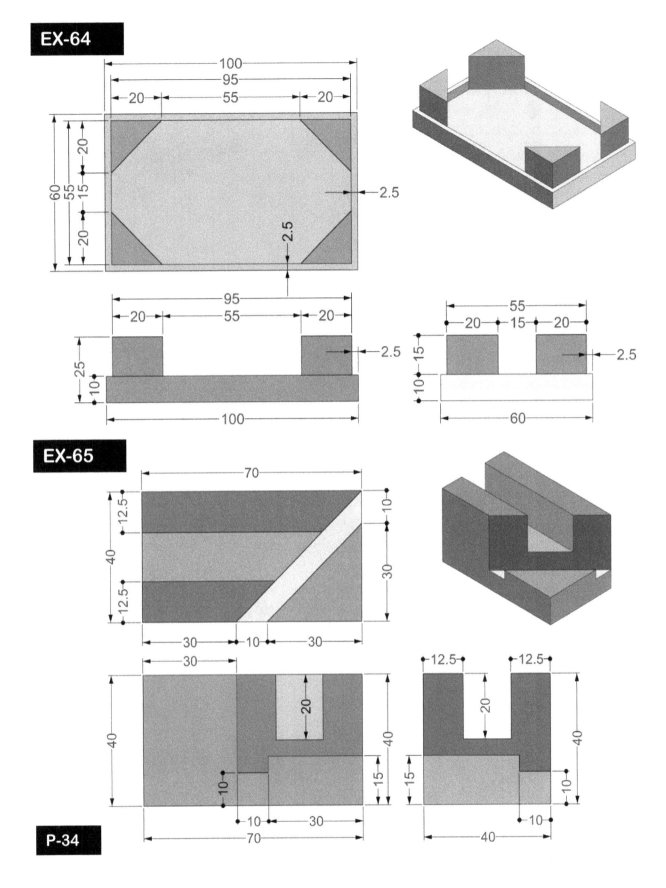

EX-64

EX-65

P-34

EX-66

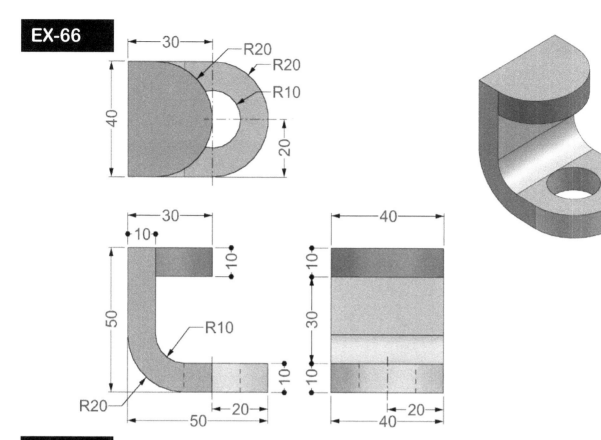

EX-67

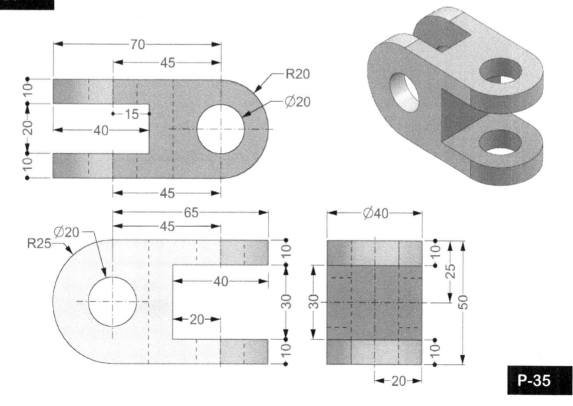

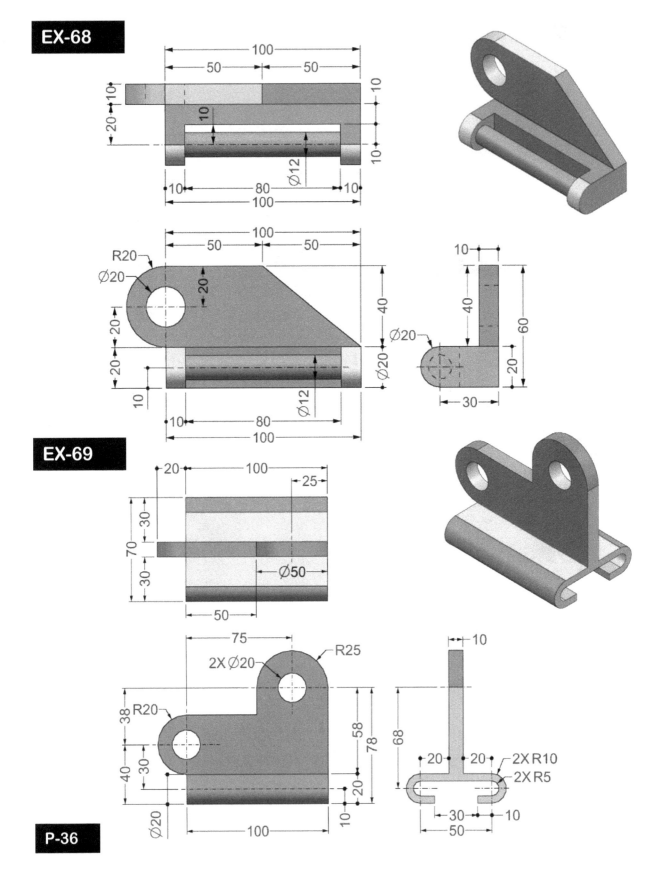

EX-68

EX-69

P-36

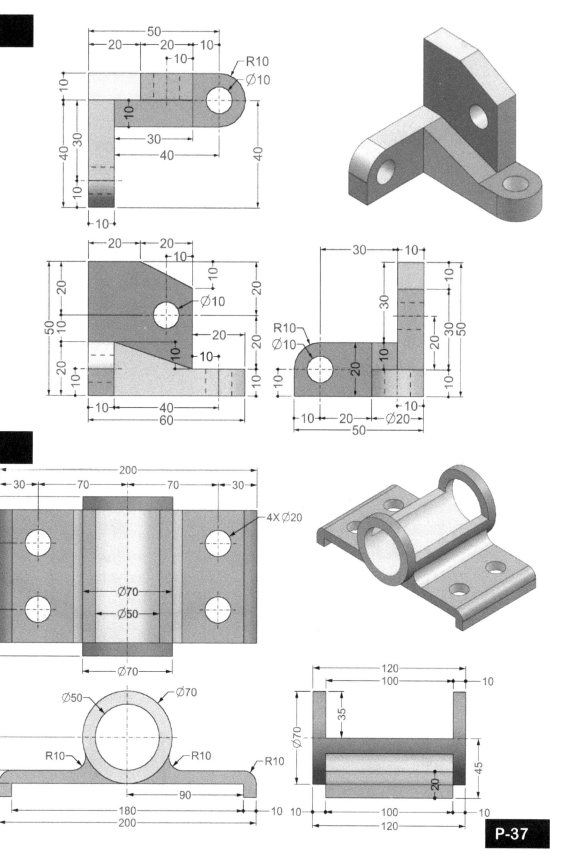

EX-70

EX-71

P-37

EX-72

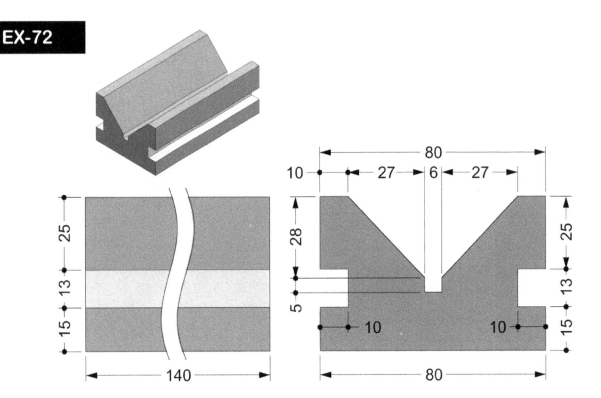

EX-73

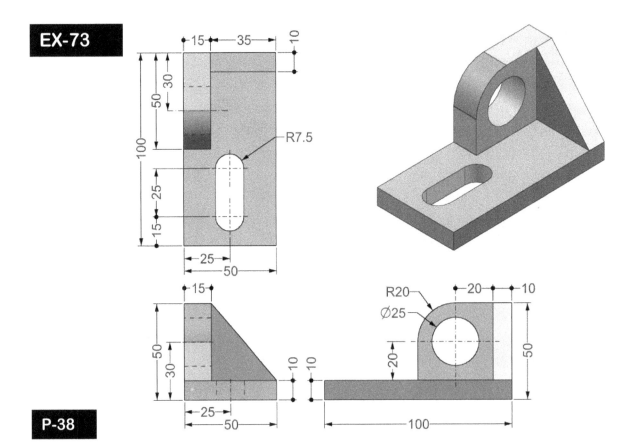

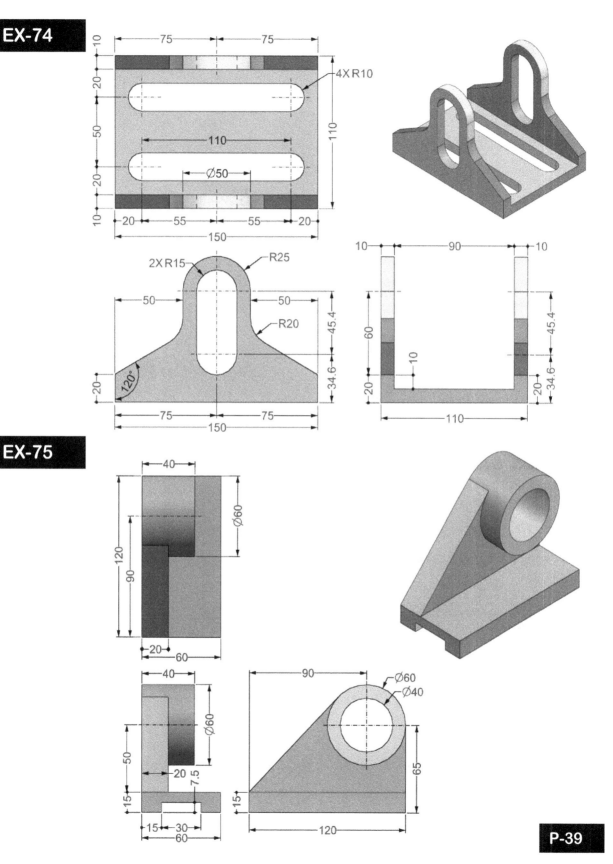

EX-75

EX-76

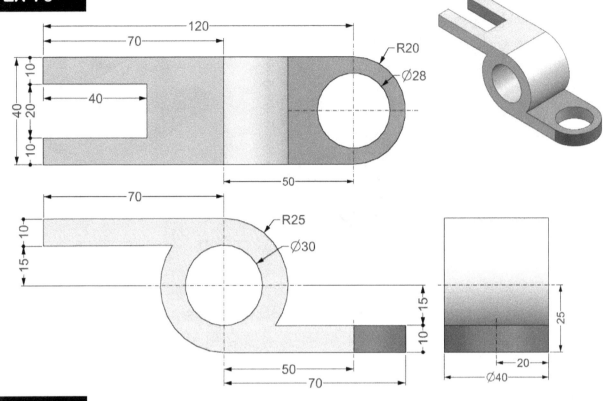

EX-77

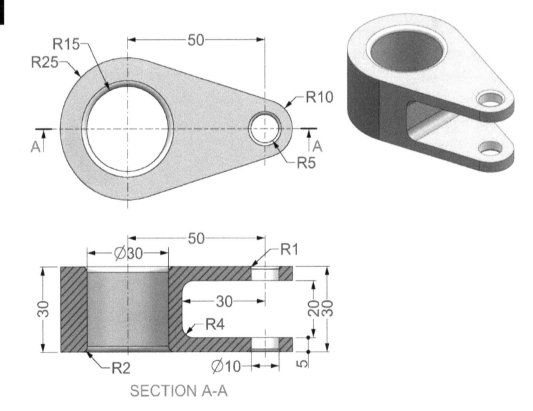

SECTION A-A

P-40

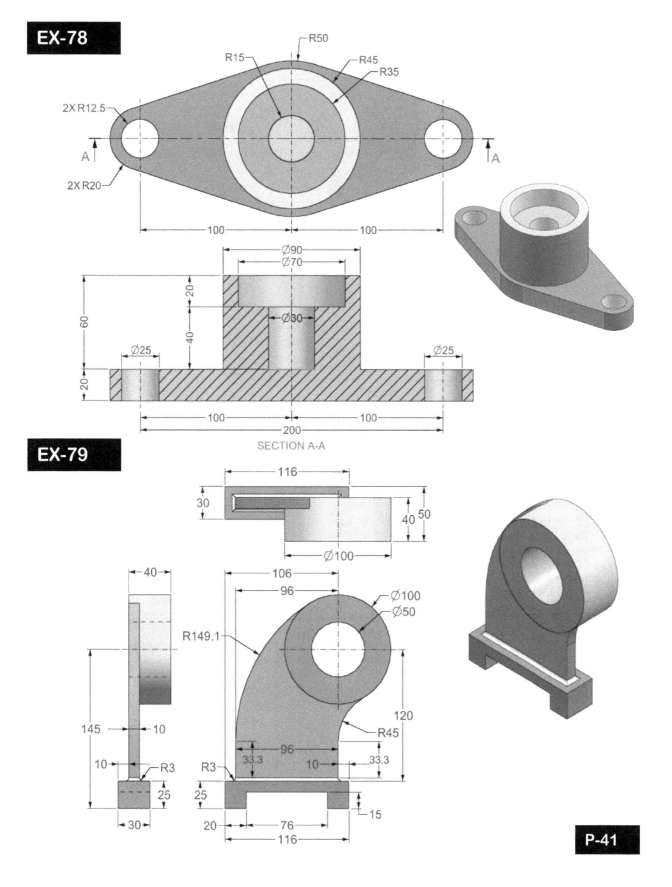

EX-78

R50
R15
R45
R35
2X R12.5
A
A
2X R20
100
100

Ø90
Ø70
20
Ø30
60
40
Ø25
Ø25
20
100
100
200

SECTION A-A

EX-79

116
30
40   50
Ø100

40
106
96
Ø100
Ø50
R149.1
120
R45
145   10
96
33.3   10   33.3
10   R3
R3
25
25
15
30
20   76
116

P-41

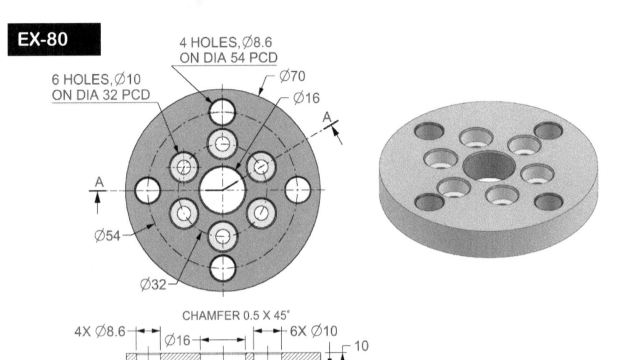

6 HOLES, ∅10 ON DIA 32 PCD

4 HOLES, ∅8.6 ON DIA 54 PCD

∅70

∅16

A

A

∅54

∅32

CHAMFER 0.5 X 45°

4X ∅8.6

∅16

6X ∅10

10

5

5

SECTION A-A
(SCALE 1:1)

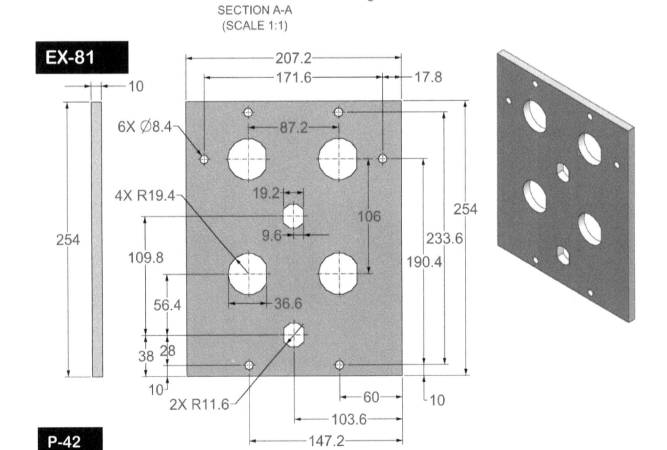

207.2

171.6

17.8

10

6X ∅8.4

87.2

4X R19.4

19.2

9.6

106

254

233.6

190.4

254

109.8

56.4

36.6

38

28

2X R11.6

10

60

10

103.6

147.2

EX-82

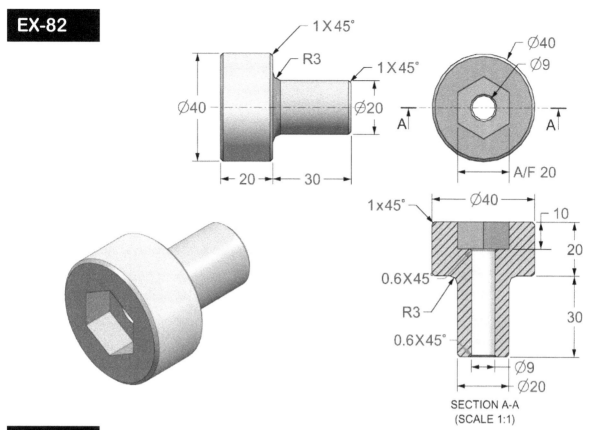

1 X 45°
R3
1 X 45°
Ø40
Ø20
20
30

Ø40
Ø9
A/F 20

1x45°
Ø40
10
20
0.6X45
R3
30
0.6X45°
Ø9
Ø20

SECTION A-A
(SCALE 1:1)

EX-83

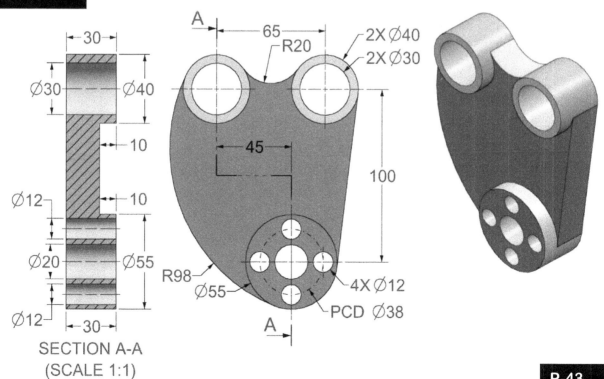

30
Ø30
Ø40
10
10
Ø12
Ø20
Ø55
Ø12
30

SECTION A-A
(SCALE 1:1)

A
65
R20
2X Ø40
2X Ø30
45
100
R98
Ø55
4X Ø12
PCD Ø38
A

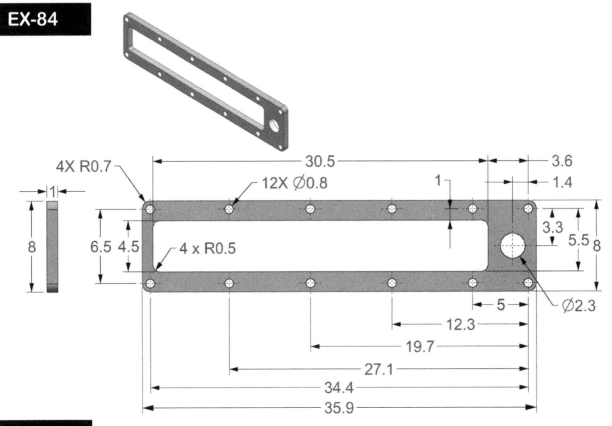

4X R0.7
12X Ø0.8
1
30.5
3.6
1.4
3.3
5.5
8
1
8
6.5 4.5
4 x R0.5
5
Ø2.3
12.3
19.7
27.1
34.4
35.9

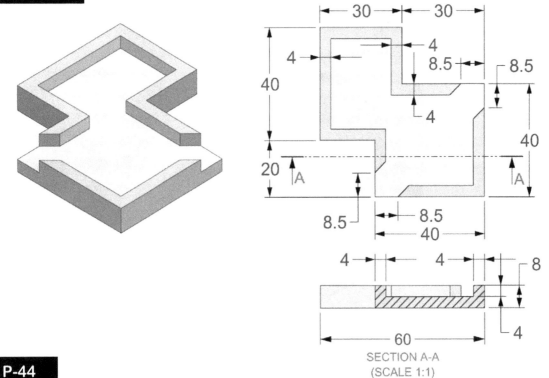

30
30
4
4
8.5
8.5
40
4
8.5
40
4
20
A
A
8.5
8.5
40
4
4
8
60
4

SECTION A-A
(SCALE 1:1)

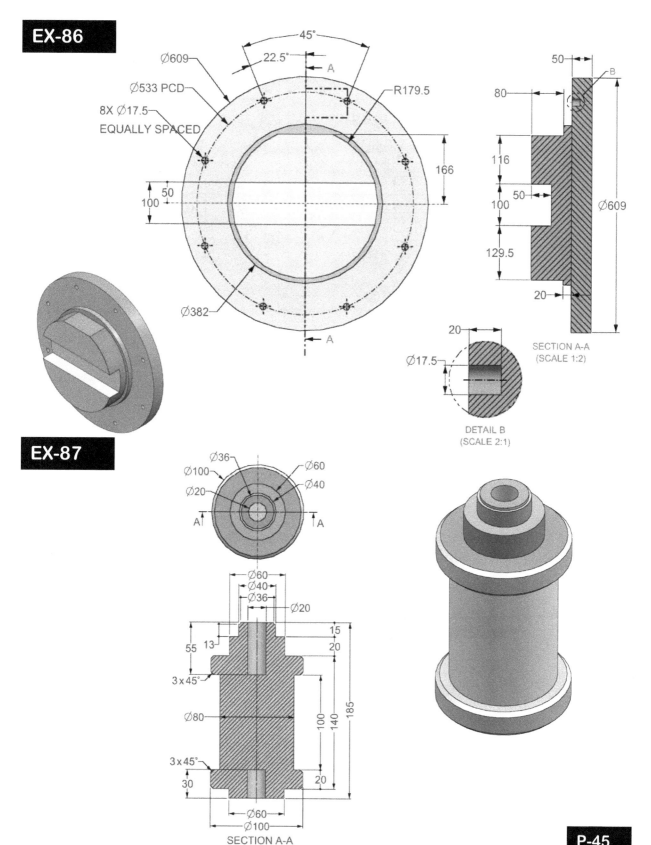

EX-86

∅609
∅533 PCD
8X ∅17.5
EQUALLY SPACED
45°
22.5°
A
R179.5
166
50
100
∅382
A

50
80
B
116
50
100
129.5
20
∅609

SECTION A-A
(SCALE 1:2)

20
∅17.5

DETAIL B
(SCALE 2:1)

EX-87

∅36
∅100
∅60
∅20
∅40
A
A

∅60
∅40
∅36
∅20
15
20
55
13
3 x 45°
100
140
185
∅80
3 x 45°
30
20
∅60
∅100

SECTION A-A

P-45

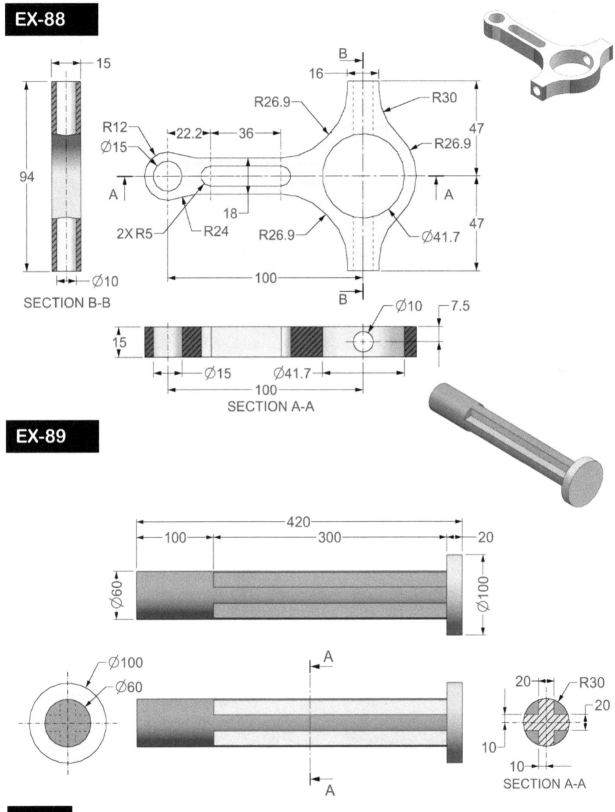

EX-88

15

94

R12
Ø15

22.2   36

R26.9

16

B

R30

47

R26.9

A

A

18

2X R5   R24   R26.9

100

Ø41.7

47

B

Ø10

SECTION B-B

15

Ø10   7.5

Ø15   Ø41.7

100

SECTION A-A

EX-89

420

100   300   20

Ø60

Ø100

Ø100
Ø60

A

A

20   R30

20

10

10

SECTION A-A

P-46

EX-90

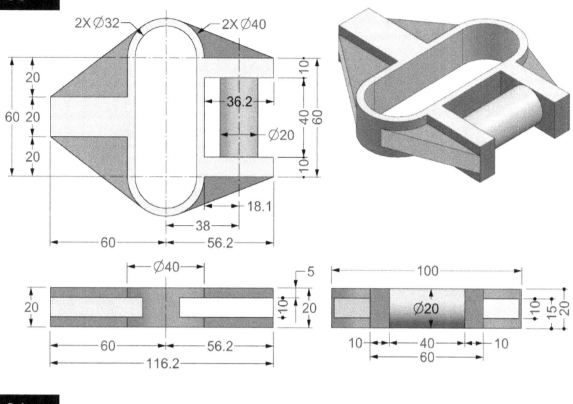

EX-91

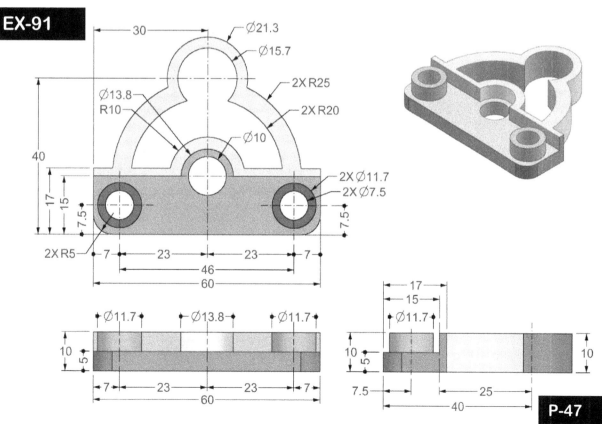

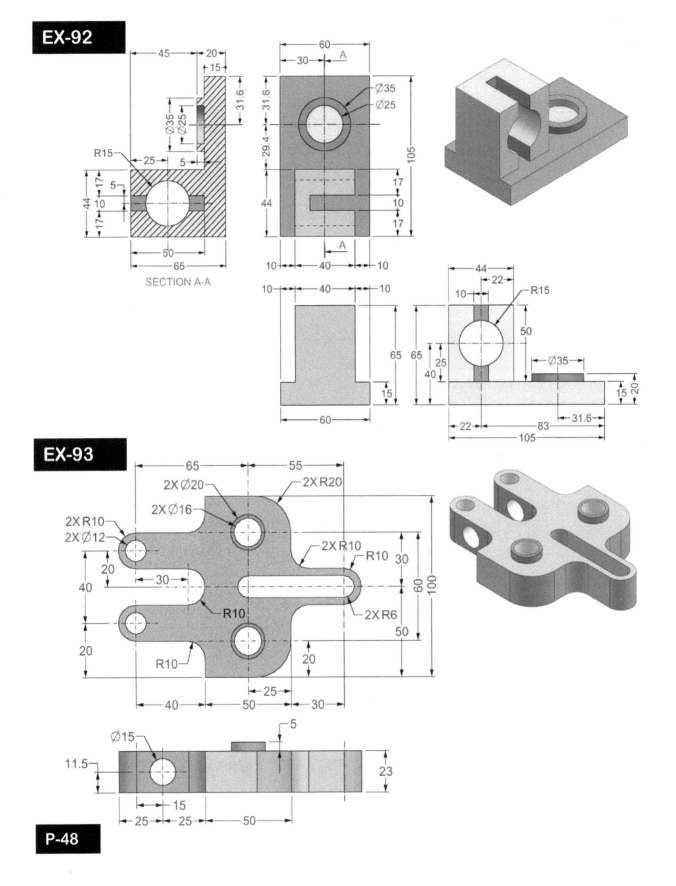

EX-92

SECTION A-A

EX-93

P-48

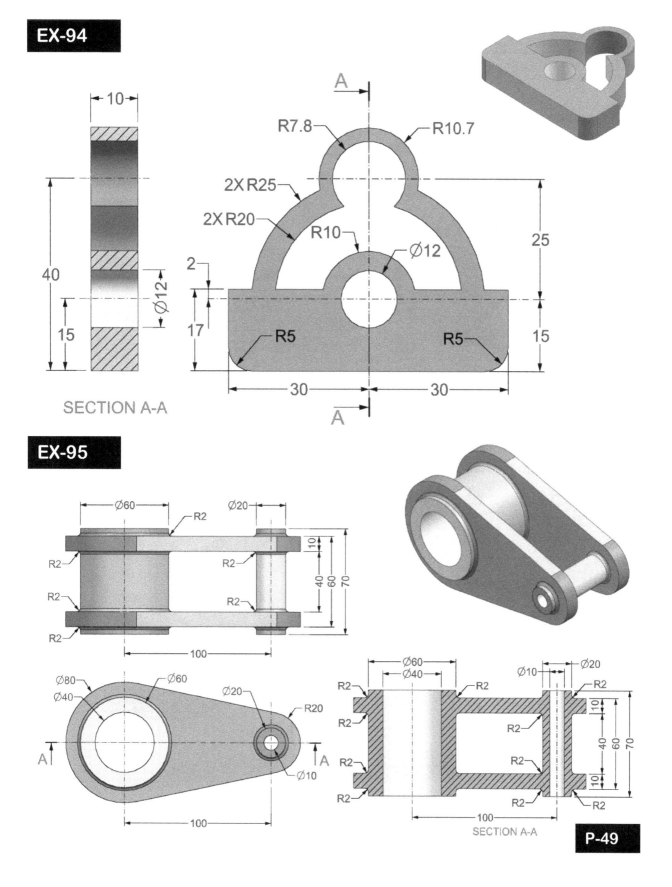

EX-94

10

40

15

Ø12

SECTION A-A

A

R7.8   R10.7

2X R25

2X R20   R10   Ø12

2   25

17   15

R5   R5

30   30

A

EX-95

Ø60   Ø20   R2

R2   R2

R2   R2

10
40
60
70

R2   R2

100

Ø80   Ø60   Ø20   R20
Ø40

A   A

Ø10

100

Ø60   Ø10   Ø20
Ø40

R2   R2   R2

R2   R2

10
40
60
70

R2   R2

R2   R2   R2

100
SECTION A-A

P-49

EX-96

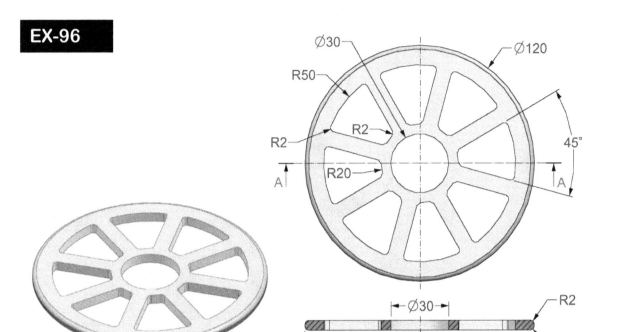

Ø30
Ø120
R50
R2
R2
R2
R20
45°
A
A

Ø30
Ø120
R2
R2
SECTION A-A

EX-97

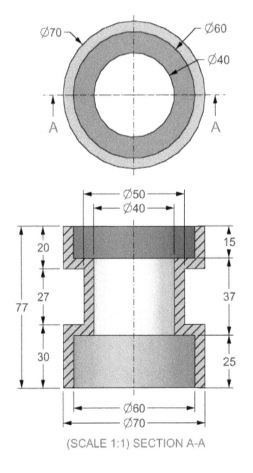

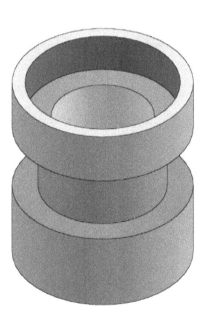

Ø70
Ø60
Ø40
A
A

Ø50
Ø40
20
15
27
37
77
30
25
Ø60
Ø70

(SCALE 1:1) SECTION A-A

P-50

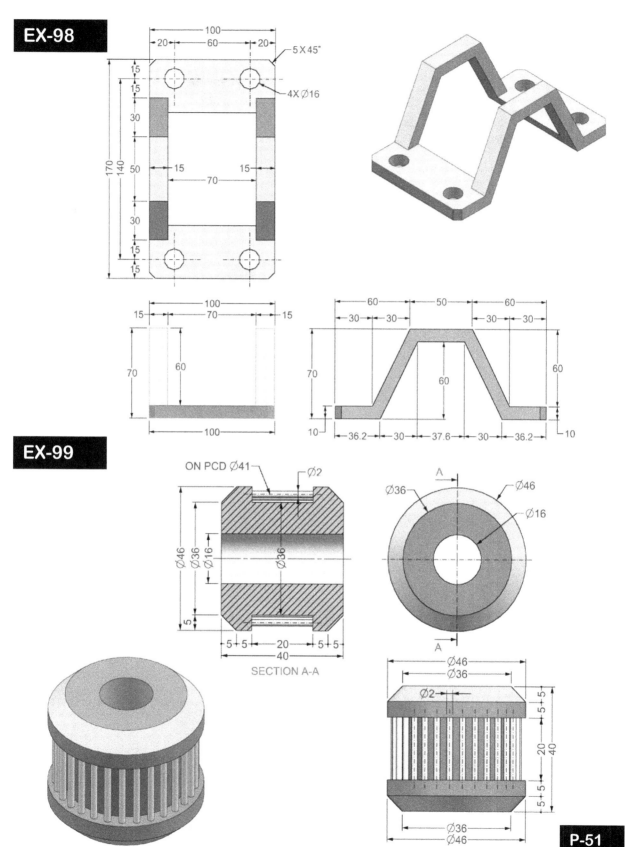

EX-98

5 X 45°
4X Ø16

100
20 60 20
15
15
30
50
15 15
70
30
15
15
170
140

100
15 70 15
70
60
100

60 50 60
30 30 30 30
70
60
60
10
36.2 30 37.6 30 36.2
10

EX-99

ON PCD Ø41
Ø2
Ø46
Ø36
Ø16
Ø36
Ø46
Ø36
Ø16
A
A
5
5 5 20 5 5
40
SECTION A-A

Ø46
Ø36
Ø2
5 5
20
5 5
40
Ø36
Ø46

P-51

EX-100

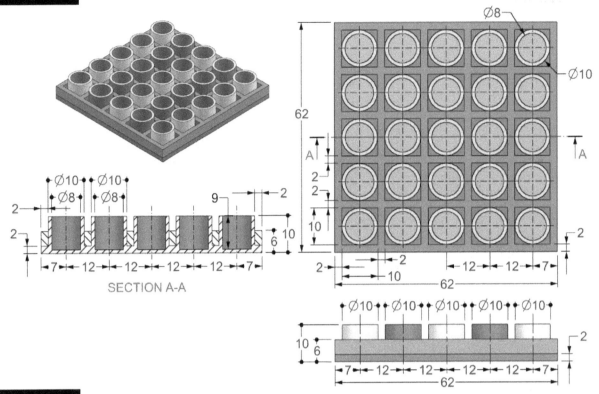

SECTION A-A

EX-101

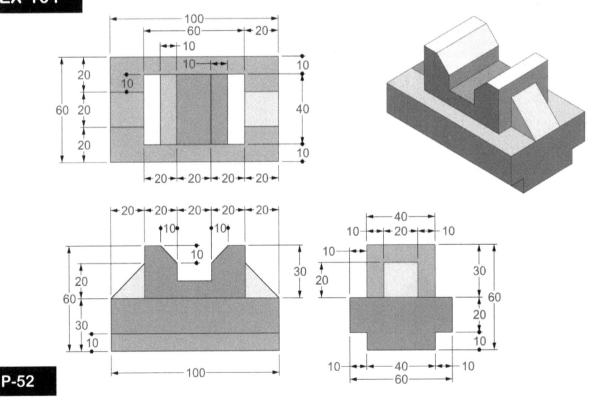

P-52

EX-102

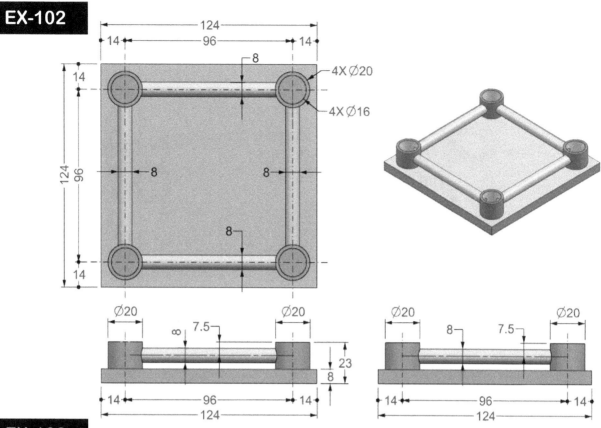

EX-103

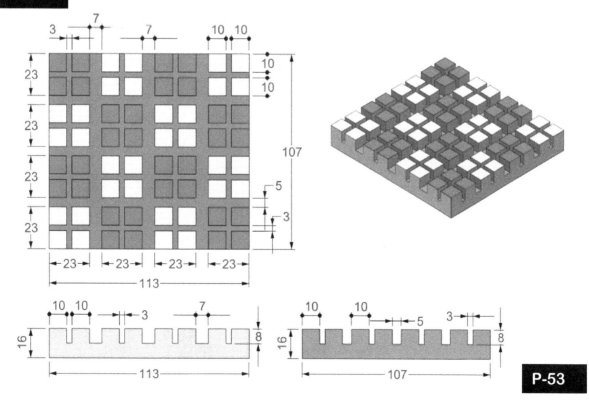

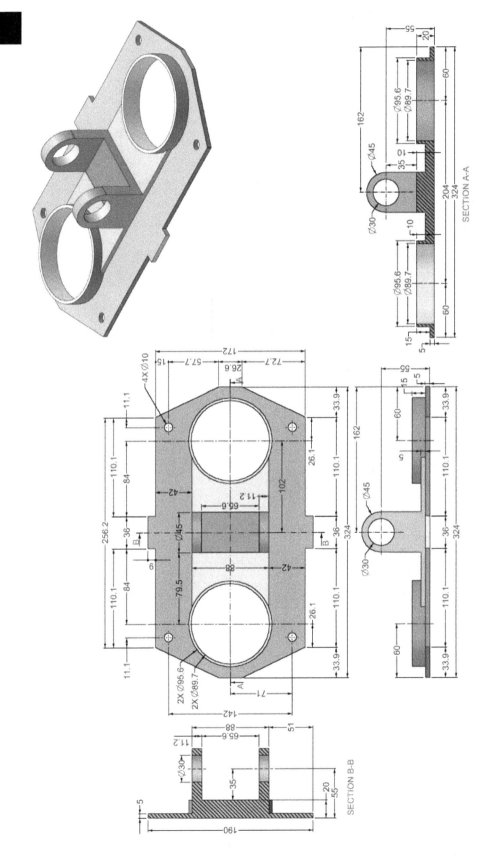

SECTION A-A

SECTION B-B

EX-105

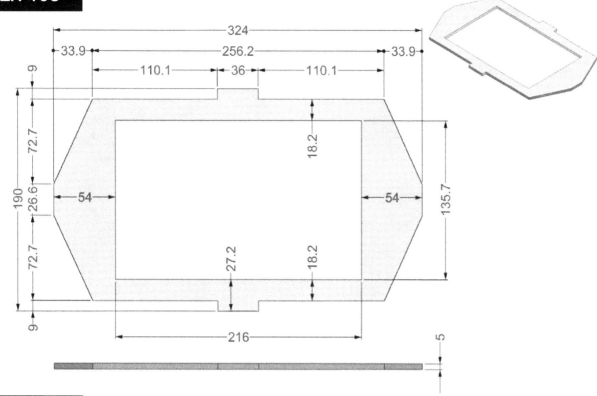

EX-106

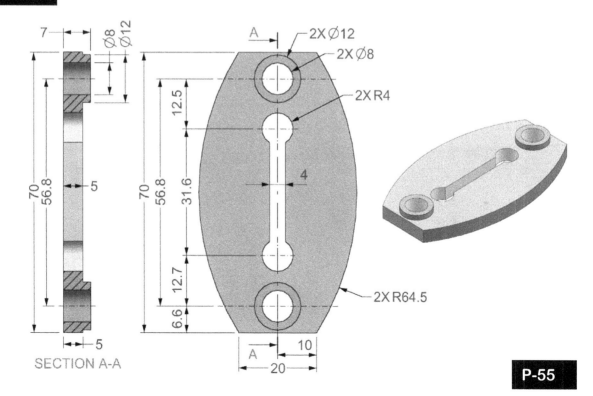

SECTION A-A

2X Ø12
2X Ø8
2X R4
2X R64.5

EX-107

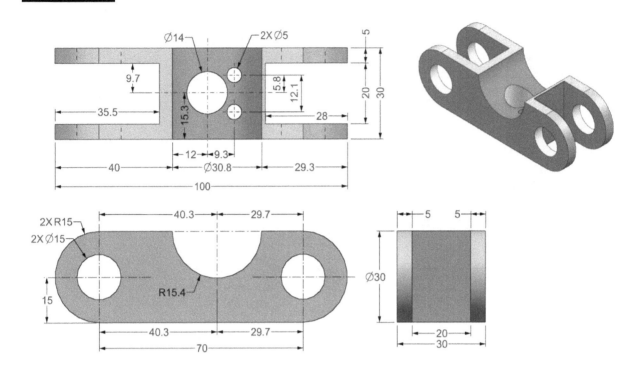

EX-108

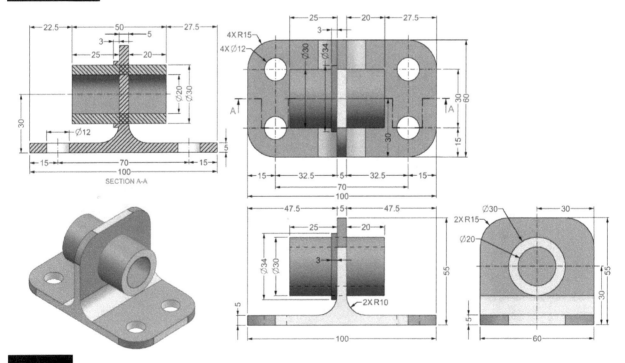

SECTION A-A

P-56

EX-109

Top view dimensions: 100, 35.5, 29, 35.5, 20.5, 20.5, 10, 5, 5, 30, 20, 20.5, 5, 19, 5, 20.5, 70

Front view dimensions: 2X R15, 2X ∅15, 5, 5, 20, 35, 35, 20.5, 20, 20.5, 19, 29, 70, 100

Side view dimensions: 2X ∅15, 2X R15, 5, 5, 20, 70, 35, ∅30, ∅15, 20, 20, 15, 30

EX-110

Front view dimensions: 29, 19, 5, 40, 25, 70, 55, ∅15, 30, 15, 14.5

Bottom view dimensions: 14.5, ∅15, 15, 30, 50, 35, 65, 20, 19, 5, 29

Side view dimensions: 55, 15, 40, 2X R15, 3X ∅15, 15, 15, 50, 35, 25, 15, 20

P-57

EX-111

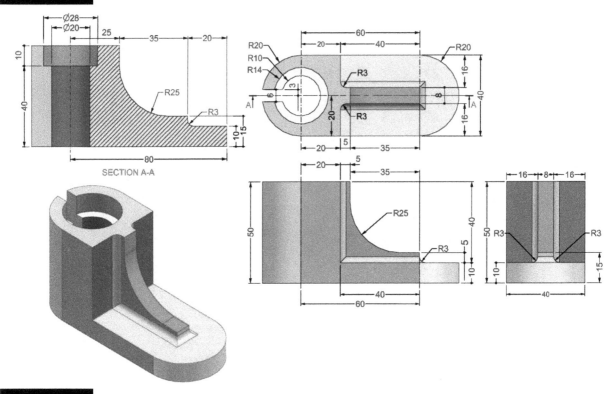

SECTION A-A

EX-112

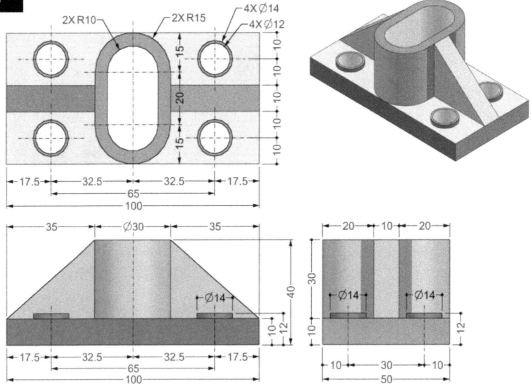

P-58

EX-113

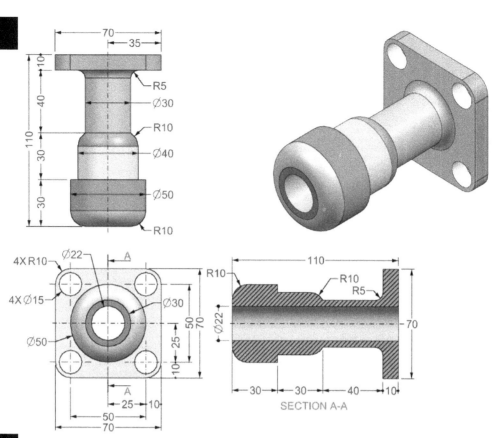

4X R10 — Ø22
4X Ø15
Ø50
Ø30
Ø22

R10
R10
R5

110
70
50
25
10
25 — 10
50
70

30 — 30 — 40 — 10

SECTION A-A

70
35
R5
Ø30
R10
Ø40
Ø50
R10
110
10
40
30
30

EX-114

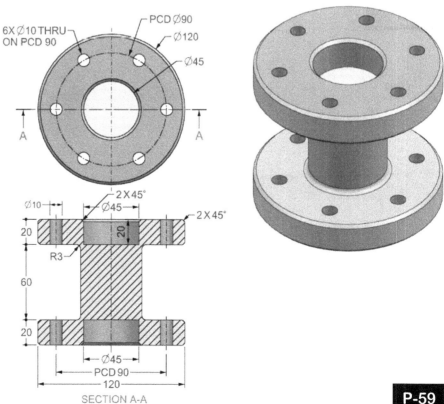

6X Ø10 THRU
ON PCD 90
PCD Ø90
Ø120
Ø45

Ø10
2 X 45°
Ø45
2 X 45°
20
20
R3
60
20
Ø45
PCD 90
120

SECTION A-A

P-59

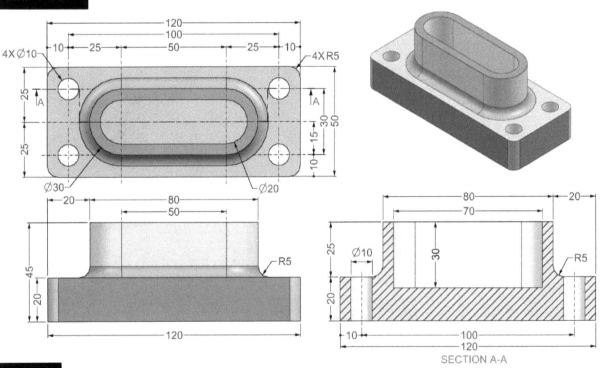

EX-115

Ø120
6X Ø10
6X Ø8
PCD Ø90
Ø68
Ø45

A   A

Ø120
Ø68   R2
Ø10   10
              10
              20

              120

              60

              20
              10
PCD 90

Ø120
PCD 90
Ø68
Ø45   Ø10

              2 X 45°

40

20   20

R3   Ø8
60   Ø55
R3   Ø50

20   20
20

Ø45   Ø8
SECTION A-A

EX-116

120
100
10   25   50   25   10
4X Ø10   4X R5

25
A   A
                                30
25   50
                                15
                                10
Ø30   Ø20

20   80
            50

45
                              R5
20

120

80   20
70

25   Ø10   30   R5

20

10   100
            120
SECTION A-A

P-60

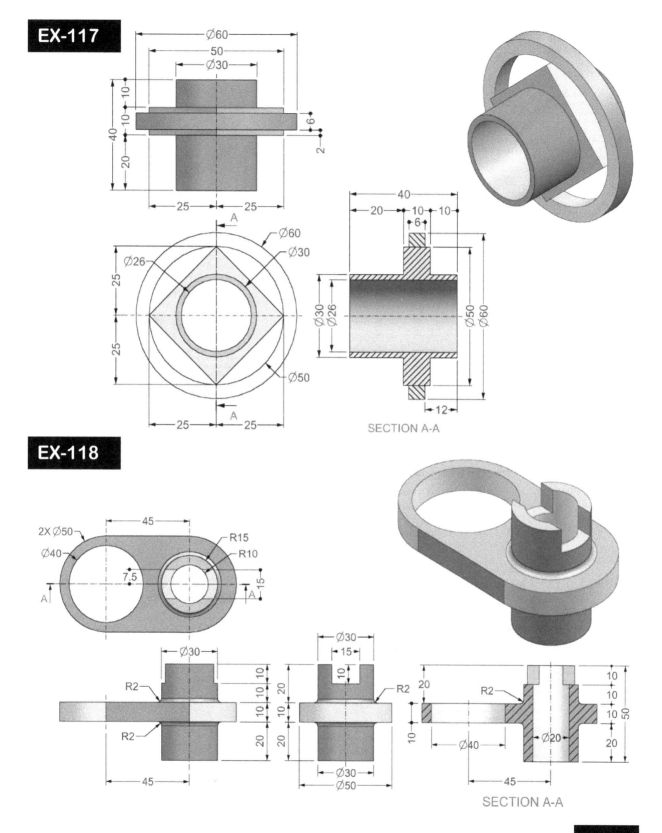

EX-117

Ø60
50
Ø30
10
10
40
20
6
2
25 25

A

Ø26
Ø60
Ø30
25
25
Ø50
25 25
A

40
20 10 10
6
Ø30
Ø26
Ø50
Ø60
12

SECTION A-A

EX-118

2X Ø50
Ø40
R15
R10
7.5
15
A
A

Ø30
R2
R2
10 10
10 10
20
45

Ø30
15
10
20
10
R2
Ø30
Ø50

20
R2
Ø40
Ø20
10
10
10
50
20
45

SECTION A-A

P-61

EX-119

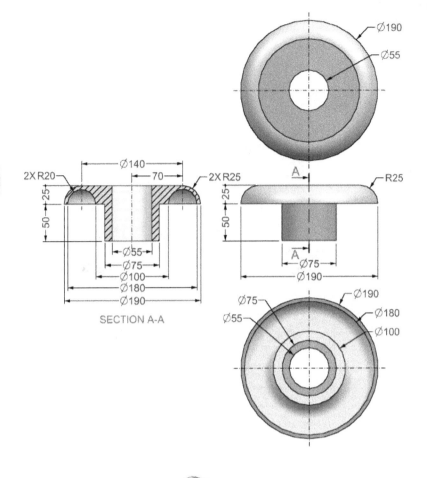

2X R20

2X R25

R25

Ø140

70

Ø190

Ø55

Ø55
Ø75
Ø100
Ø180
Ø190

25
50

SECTION A-A

A

25
50

Ø75
Ø190

A

Ø75
Ø55
Ø190
Ø180
Ø100

EX-120

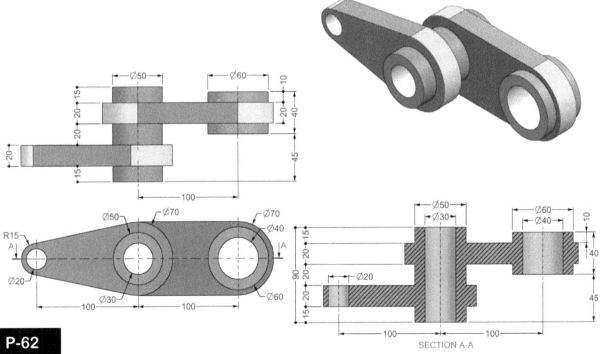

Ø50
Ø60
10
15
20
20
20
40
20
15
20
100

Ø50
Ø70
Ø70
Ø40
R15
A
Ø50
Ø30
Ø60
Ø20
100
100
A

Ø50
Ø30
Ø60
Ø40
10
15
20
20
20
40
Ø20
90
15
45
100
100

SECTION A-A

P-62

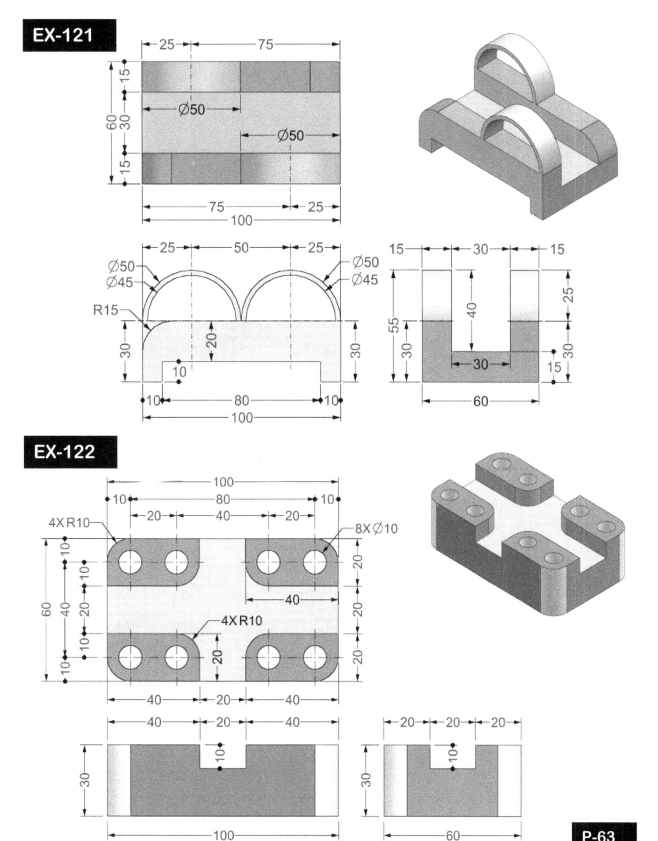

EX-121

EX-122

P-63

EX-123

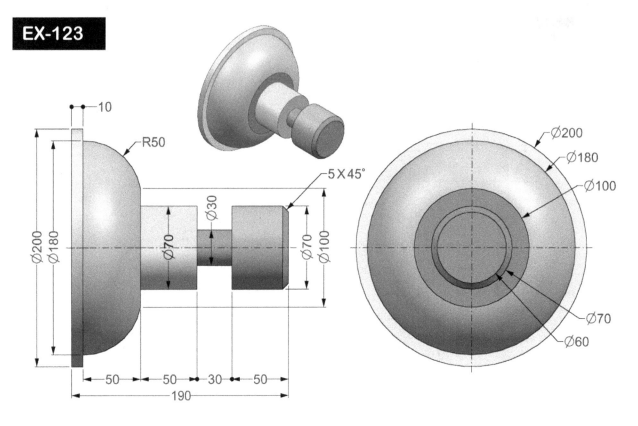

- 10
- R50
- 5 X 45°
- Ø30
- Ø70
- Ø70
- Ø100
- Ø200
- Ø180
- 50
- 50
- 30
- 50
- 190
- Ø200
- Ø180
- Ø100
- Ø70
- Ø60

EX-124

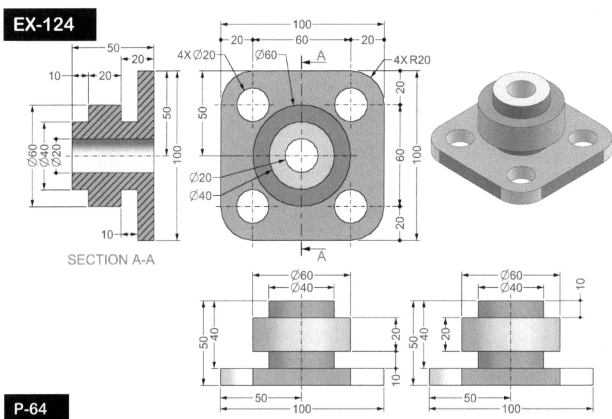

- 50
- 20
- 10
- 20
- Ø60
- Ø40
- Ø20
- 50
- 100
- 10
- SECTION A-A
- 100
- 20
- 60
- 20
- 4X Ø20
- Ø60
- A
- 4X R20
- 20
- 50
- 60
- 100
- Ø20
- Ø40
- 20
- A
- Ø60
- Ø40
- 50
- 40
- 50
- 100
- 20
- 10
- Ø60
- Ø40
- 10
- 50
- 40
- 20
- 50
- 100

P-64

EX-125

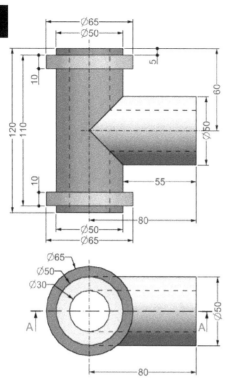

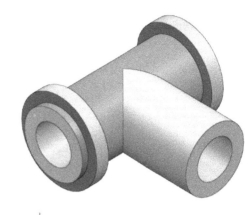

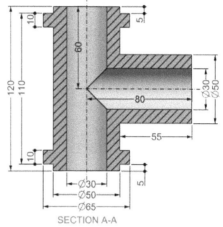

SECTION A-A

EX-126

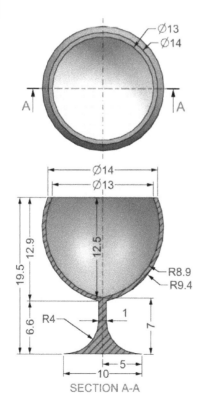

SECTION A-A

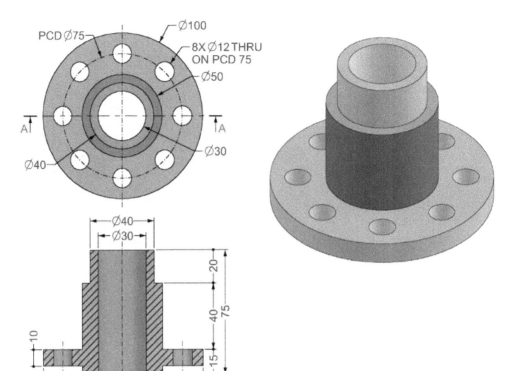

PCD Ø75

Ø100

8X Ø12 THRU
ON PCD 75

Ø50

Ø30

A

A

Ø40

Ø40
Ø30

20

75

40

10

15

Ø50

75

Ø100

SECTION A-A

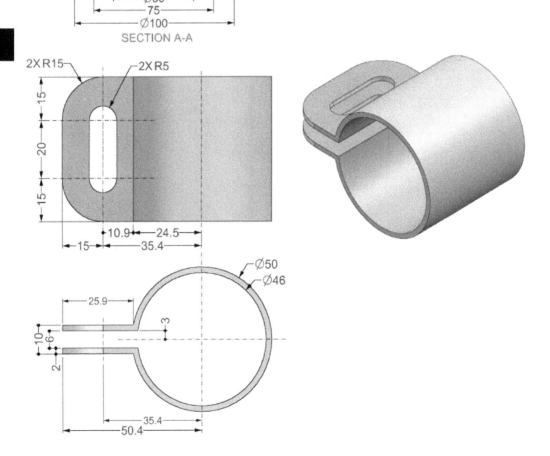

2X R15

2X R5

15

20

15

10.9   24.5

15   35.4

Ø50
Ø46

25.9

3

10
6

2

35.4
50.4

EX-129

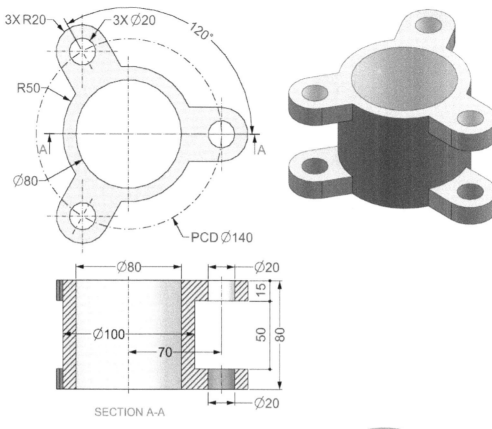

3X R20 3X Ø20 120°
R50
Ø80
PCD Ø140

Ø80 Ø20
15
Ø100 50 80
70
Ø20

SECTION A-A

EX-130

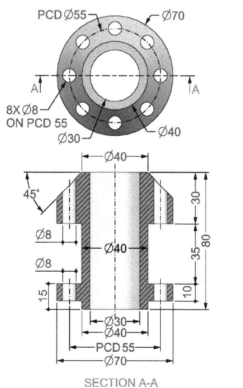

PCD Ø55 Ø70
8X Ø8
ON PCD 55
Ø30 Ø40

Ø40
45°
Ø8
Ø40
Ø8
30
80
35
15
10
Ø30
Ø40
PCD 55
Ø70

SECTION A-A

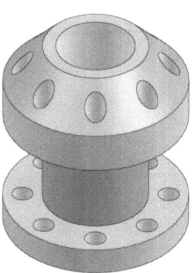

EX-131

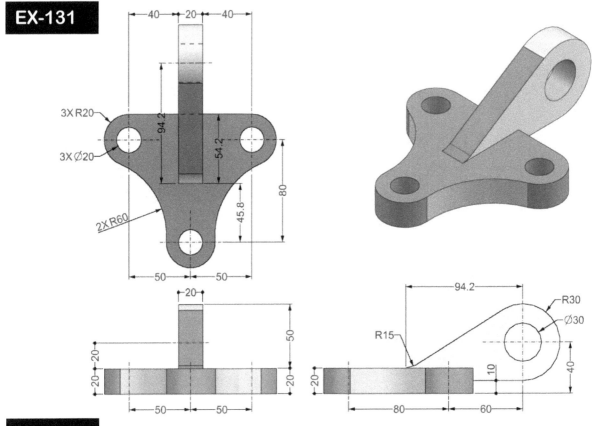

EX-132

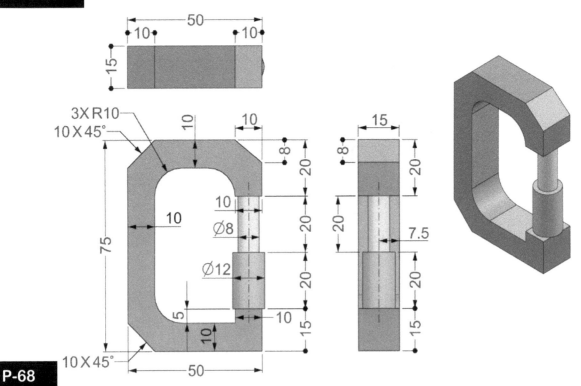

EX-133

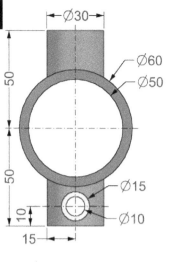

⌀30

⌀60
⌀50

50
50

⌀15
⌀10

10
15

⌀30 ⌀15 ⌀20

36
40
18
20

30
⌀60

⌀15 ⌀60
30

18
36
⌀30
40
⌀30

10 40 50 20

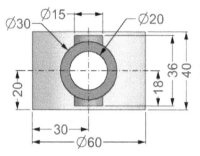

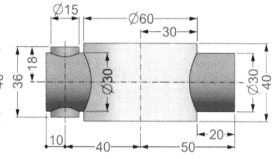

EX-134

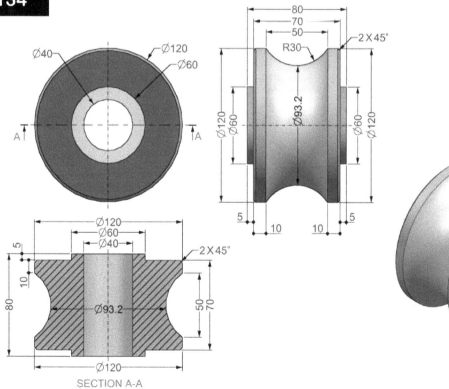

⌀40 ⌀120
⌀60

A A

80
70
50
R30
2 X 45°

⌀120
⌀60
⌀93.2
⌀60
⌀120

5 5
10 10

⌀120
⌀60
⌀40

5
10
2 X 45°

80
⌀93.2
50
70

⌀120

SECTION A-A

P-69

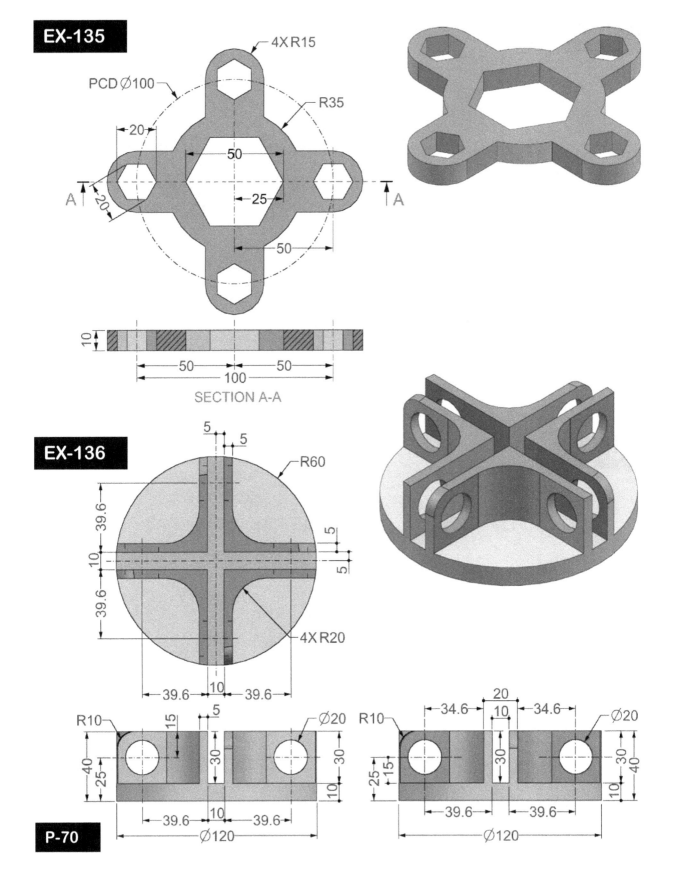

EX-135

4X R15
PCD ⌀100
R35
20
50
25
50
A
20
20
A

10
50
50
100

SECTION A-A

EX-136

5
5
R60
39.6
5
10
5
39.6
4X R20
39.6
10
39.6

R10
15
5
⌀20
40
25
30
30
10
39.6
10
39.6
⌀120

20
10
34.6
34.6
R10
⌀20
25
15
30
40
10
39.6
39.6
⌀120

P-70

EX-137

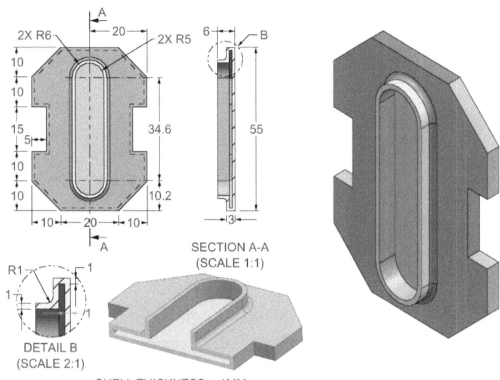

2X R6
2X R5
20
10
10
15
5
10
10
34.6
10.2
10
20
10

6
B
55
3

SECTION A-A
(SCALE 1:1)

R1
1
1
1
1

DETAIL B
(SCALE 2:1)

SHELL THICKNESS = 1MM
ALL INSIDE WALL THICKNESS

EX-138

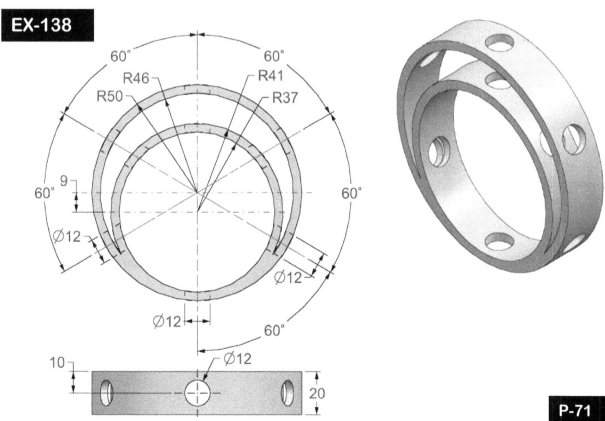

60°
60°
R46
R41
R50
R37
60°
9
60°
Ø12
Ø12
Ø12
60°
Ø12

10
Ø12
20

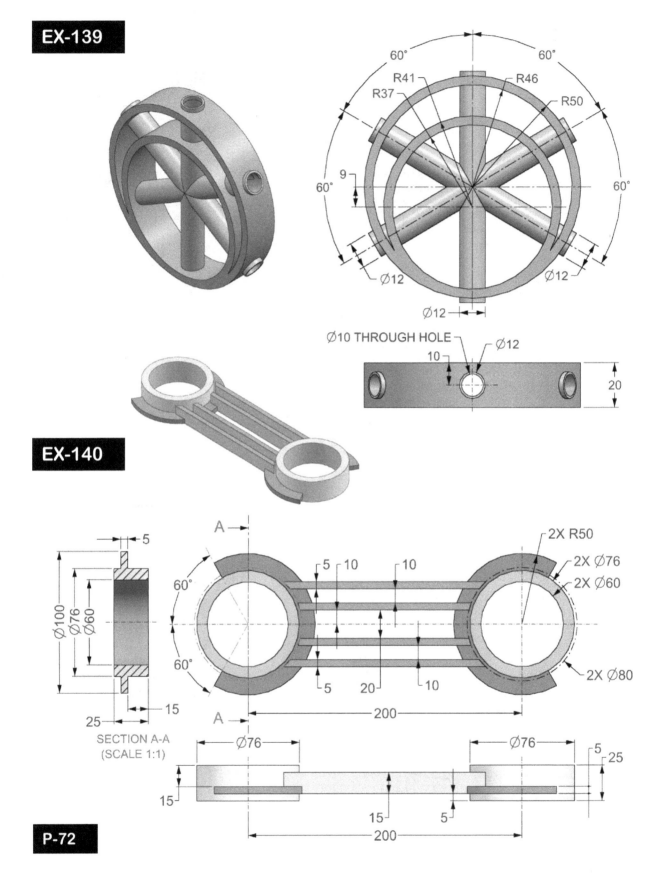

EX-139

60°   60°

R41   R46

R37

R50

60°   9   60°

Ø12   Ø12

Ø12

Ø10 THROUGH HOLE   Ø12

10

20

EX-140

A

2X R50

2X Ø76

2X Ø60

5   10   10

60°

Ø100
Ø76
Ø60

60°

5   20   10

2X Ø80

A

200

15

25

SECTION A-A
(SCALE 1:1)

Ø76   Ø76

5
25

15   15   5

200

P-72

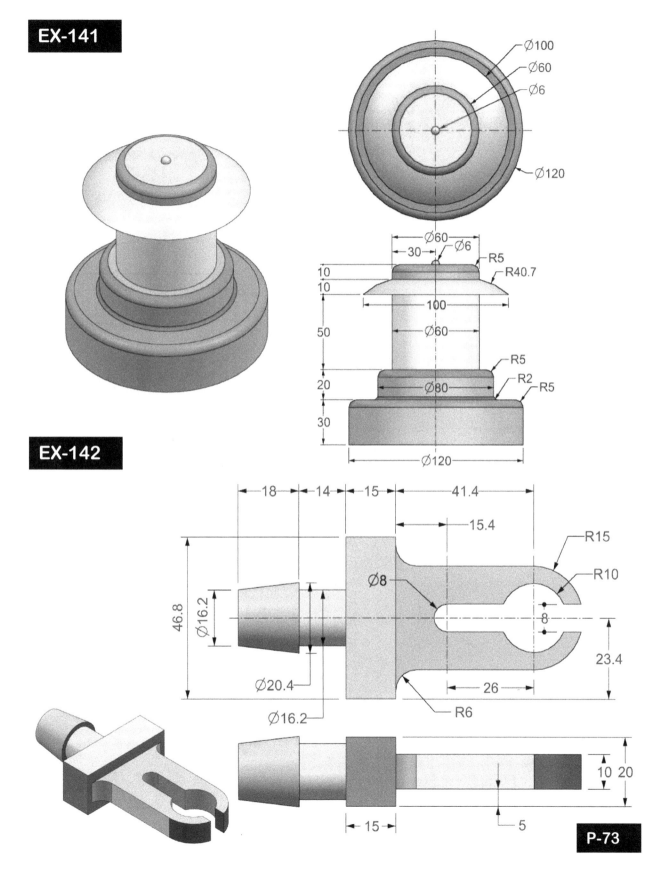

EX-141

⌀100
⌀60
⌀6
⌀120

⌀60
30
⌀6
R5
R40.7
10
10
100
⌀60
50
R5
20
⌀80
R2
R5
30
⌀120

EX-142

18
14
15
41.4
15.4
R15
R10
46.8
⌀16.2
⌀8
8
⌀20.4
23.4
26
R6
⌀16.2

15
10 20
5

P-73

EX-143

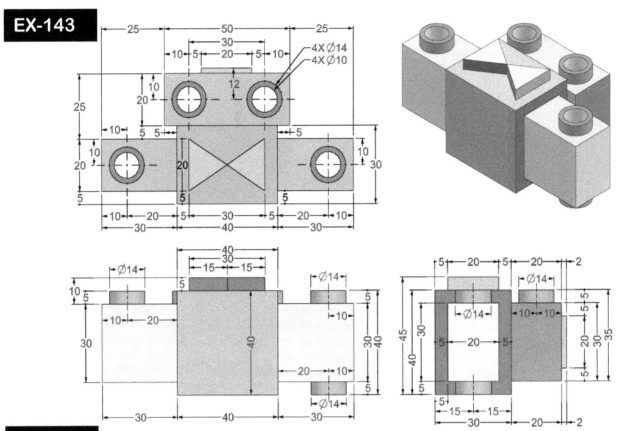

EX-144

8X Ø26 THRU HOLE
ON PCD 160

PCD Ø160

Ø80

Ø60

SECTION A-A

8X Ø12

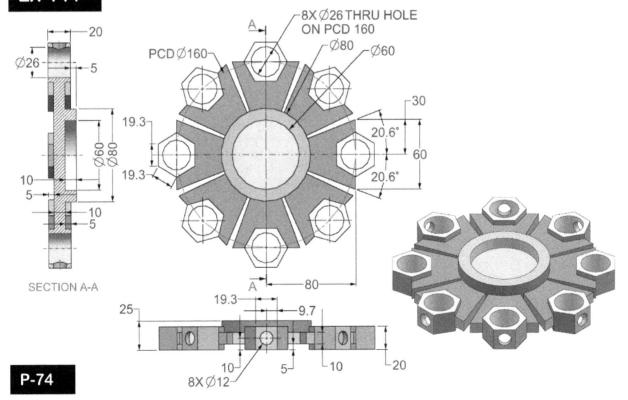

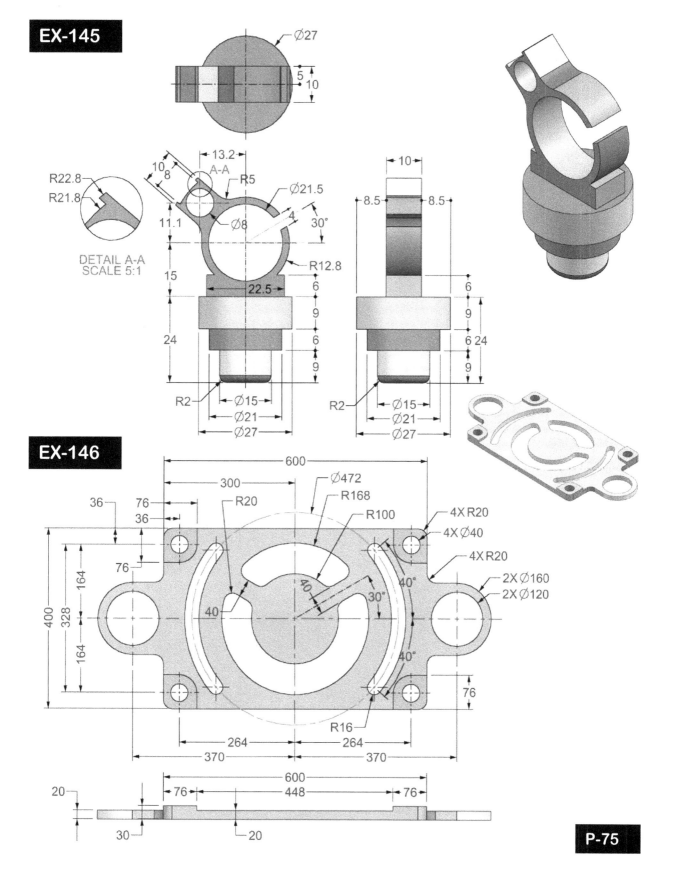

EX-145

Ø27
5
10

A-A
R22.8
R21.8
13.2
10
8
R5
Ø21.5
11.1
Ø8
4
30°
R12.8
DETAIL A-A
SCALE 5:1
15
22.5
6
24
9
6
9
R2
Ø15
Ø21
Ø27

10
8.5
8.5
6
9
6 24
9
R2
Ø15
Ø21
Ø27

EX-146

600
300
Ø472
R168
R100
4X R20
4X Ø40
36
76
36
4X R20
76
R20
40
40
2X Ø160
2X Ø120
164
40°
400
328
40°
30°
164
40
R16
76
264
264
370
370

600
76
448
76
20
30
20

P-75

Ø40
120°
Ø20
120°
10
60

R10
Ø40
200
79.6
Ø20
15
60
R15

2X Ø100
2X Ø80
Ø50
R45
R40
51.6
Ø30
A
A
100
100

Ø90
Ø50
10
10
40
15
100
100

Ø90
Ø80
Ø50
Ø30
Ø80
Ø80
15
10
10
100
100
40
15

SECTION A-A

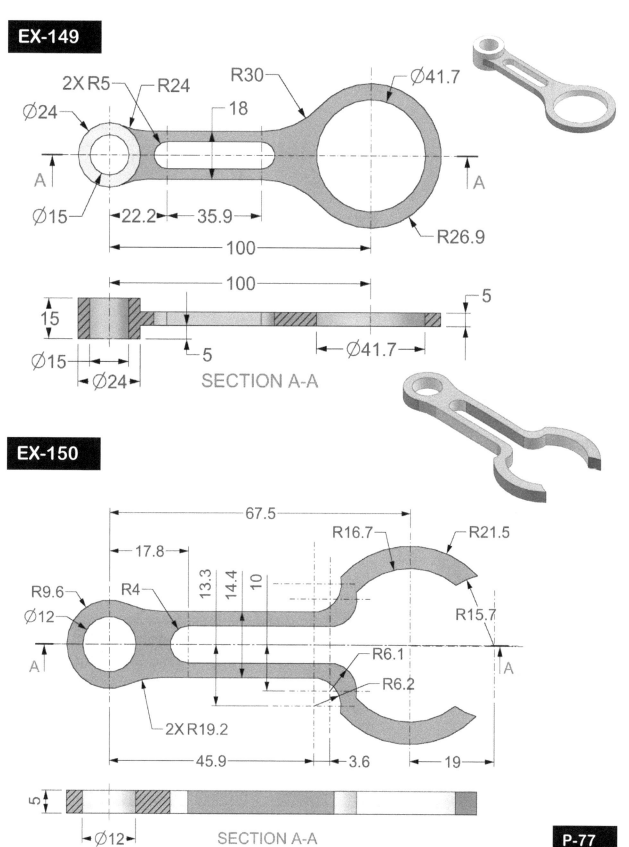

EX-149

2X R5 R24 R30 Ø41.7
Ø24 18
2X R5
R24
Ø15
A
A
Ø24
22.2 35.9
100
R26.9

100
15
5
15
5
Ø15
Ø24
Ø41.7
SECTION A-A

EX-150

67.5
17.8
13.3 14.4 10
R16.7 R21.5
R9.6
R4
Ø12
R15.7
R6.1
R6.2
A
A
2X R19.2
45.9 3.6 19

5
Ø12
SECTION A-A

P-77

Ø8

6,5

10

28

11

R1.5

R1.5

B-B

27

Ø10

SECTION A-A

Ø20

A

R3

35

15°

20

5

A

Ø13.3

Ø16

R10

R8

R6.7

R4

R5

1

45°

DETAIL B-B
SCALE 5:1

Ø20

Ø36

Ø58

Ø52

Ø16

Ø36

Ø20

R8

8

20

2

135°

13.5

Ø16

R11.2

15.8

76

21.6

10.7

13

10

R6

Ø16

R3

SECTION A-A

A

58

3

R3

R2

Ø52

76

R6

A

40

EX-153

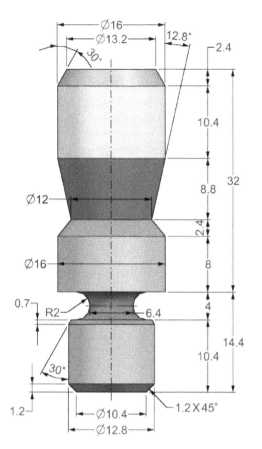

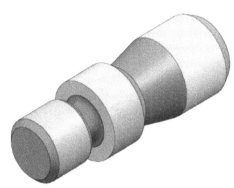

EX-154

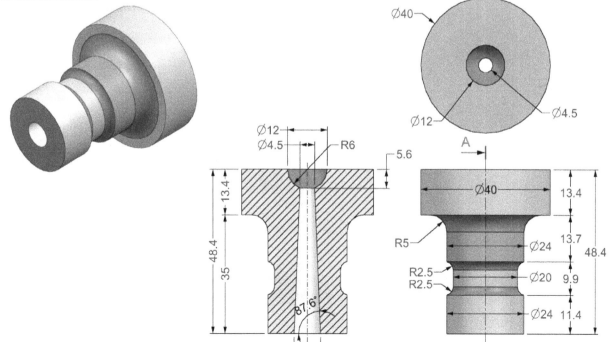

SECTION A-A

P-79

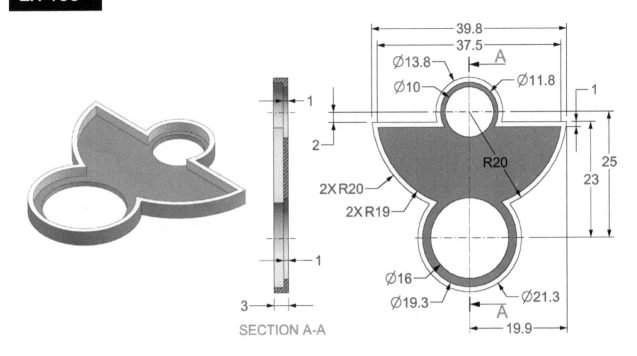

SECTION A-A

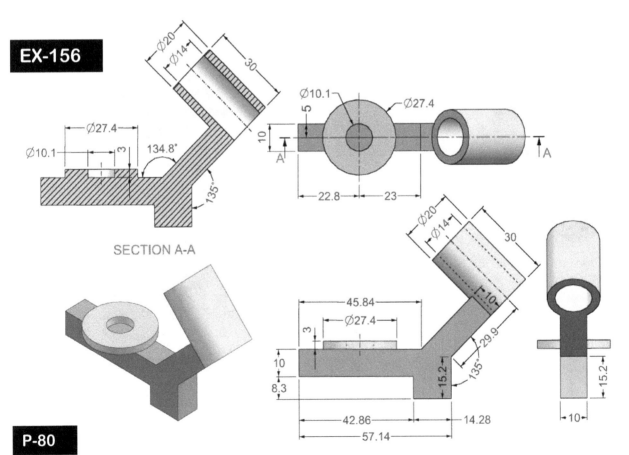

SECTION A-A

EX-157

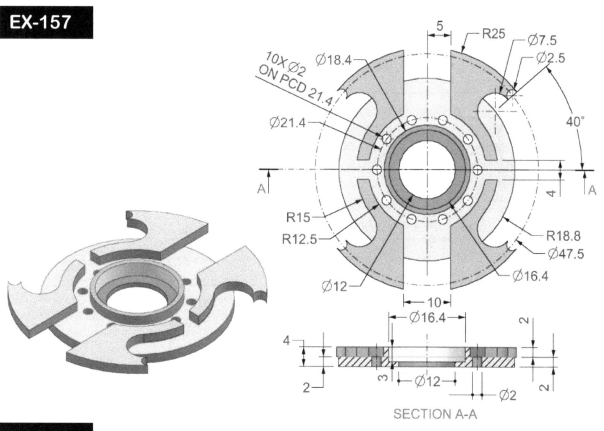

SECTION A-A

EX-158

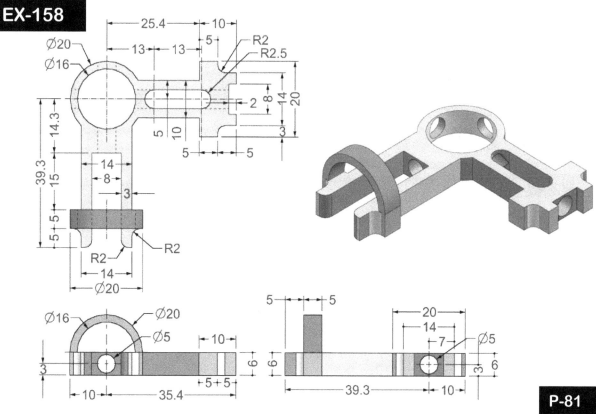

P-81

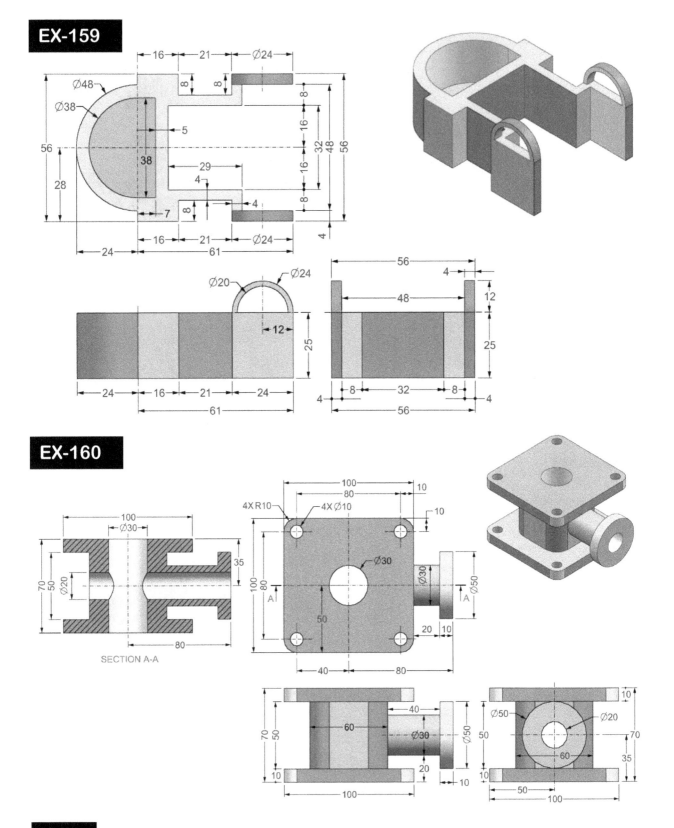

EX-159

EX-160

SECTION A-A

P-82

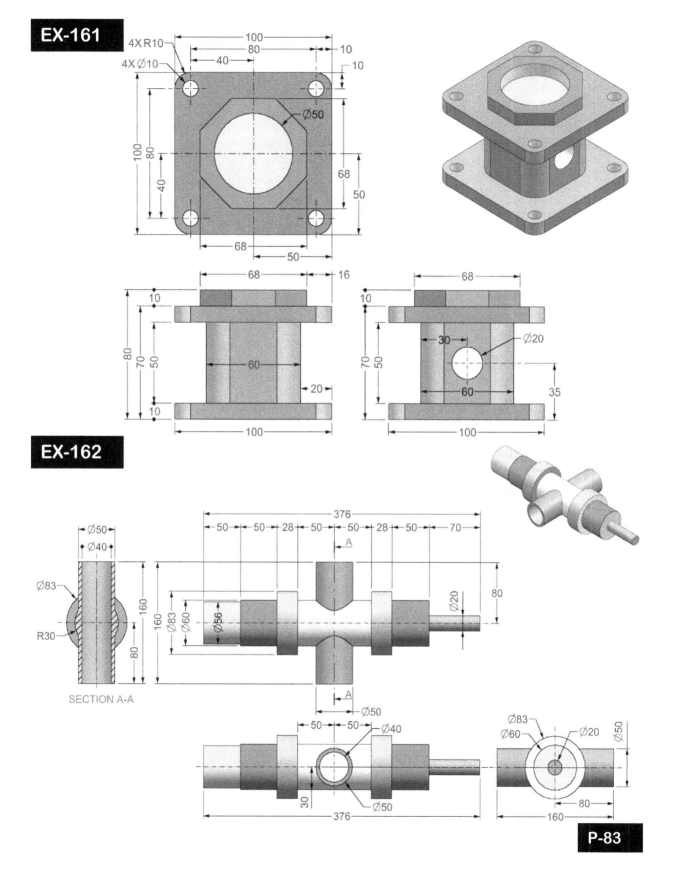

EX-161

EX-162

SECTION A-A

P-83

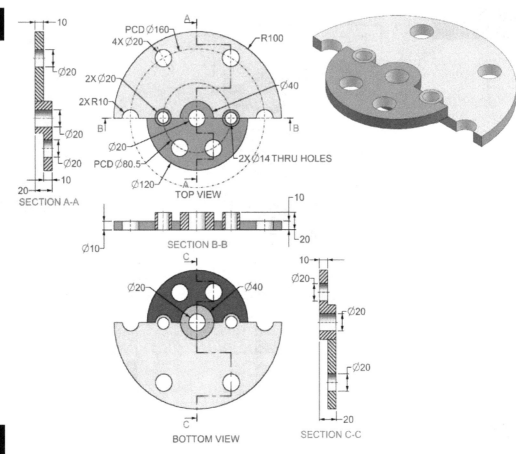

10
Ø20
Ø20
Ø20
10
20
SECTION A-A

PCD Ø160
4X Ø20
2X Ø20
2X R10
Ø20
PCD Ø80.5
Ø120
A
A
B
B
R100
Ø40
2X Ø14 THRU HOLES
TOP VIEW

10
20
Ø10
SECTION B-B

C
Ø20
Ø40
C
BOTTOM VIEW

10
Ø20
Ø20
Ø20
20
SECTION C-C

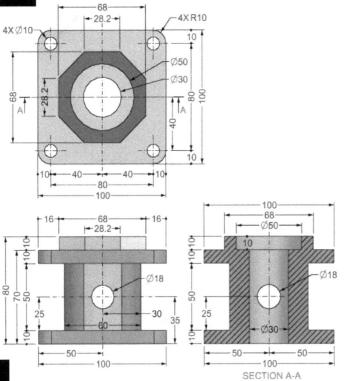

68
28.2
4X R10
4X Ø10
10
Ø50
Ø30
68
28.2
A
A
10
40
80
100
10
10
40
40
10
80
100

16
68
16
28.2
10 10
80
70
50
25
10
Ø18
30
60
35
50
100

100
68
Ø50
10 10
10
Ø18
50
25
10
Ø30
50
50
100
SECTION A-A

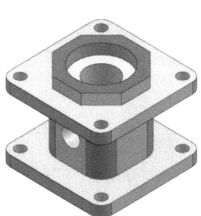

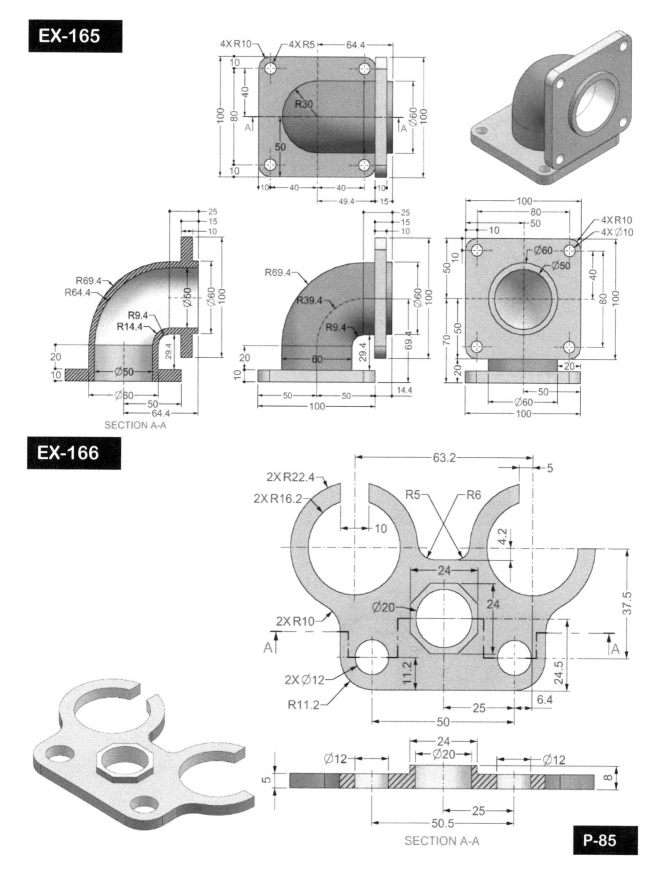

EX-165

SECTION A-A

EX-166

SECTION A-A

P-85

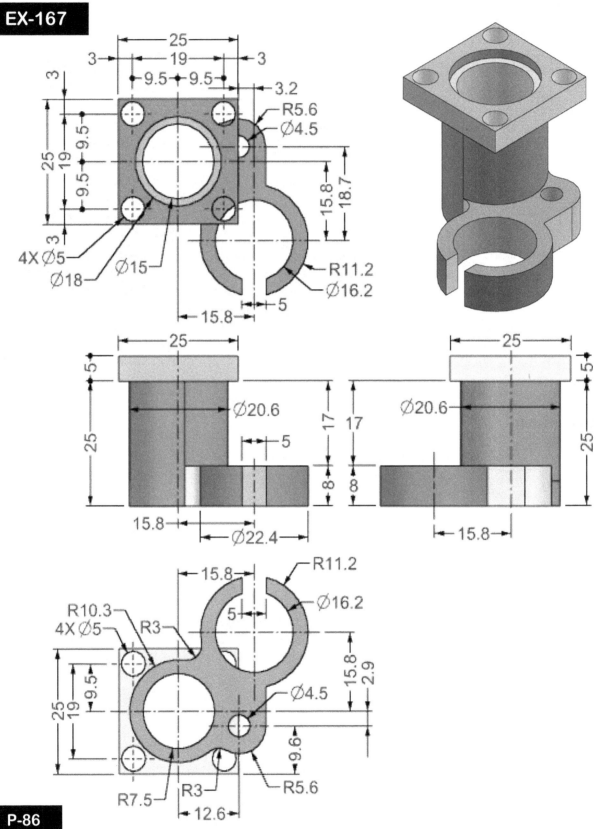

EX-168

PCD Ø95
Ø120
8X Ø14
8X Ø10
ON PCD 95
R35
R25
6
3
A
A

32
30
80 16
32
20
2
Ø70
Ø120

30
Ø14
Ø10
16 20
Ø50
Ø70
PCD 95
Ø120

SECTION A-A

EX-169

Ø70
Ø40
20
40
R5
Ø28
Ø40
50
130
70
200

Ø70
R2
R60
Ø80
R5
30
21.3
40
50
80
140
30
Ø28
Ø40
10
50
80
70

Ø70
15 40 15
10
30
30
Ø28
Ø40
80
15 15
70
30
10
35
Ø70

P-87

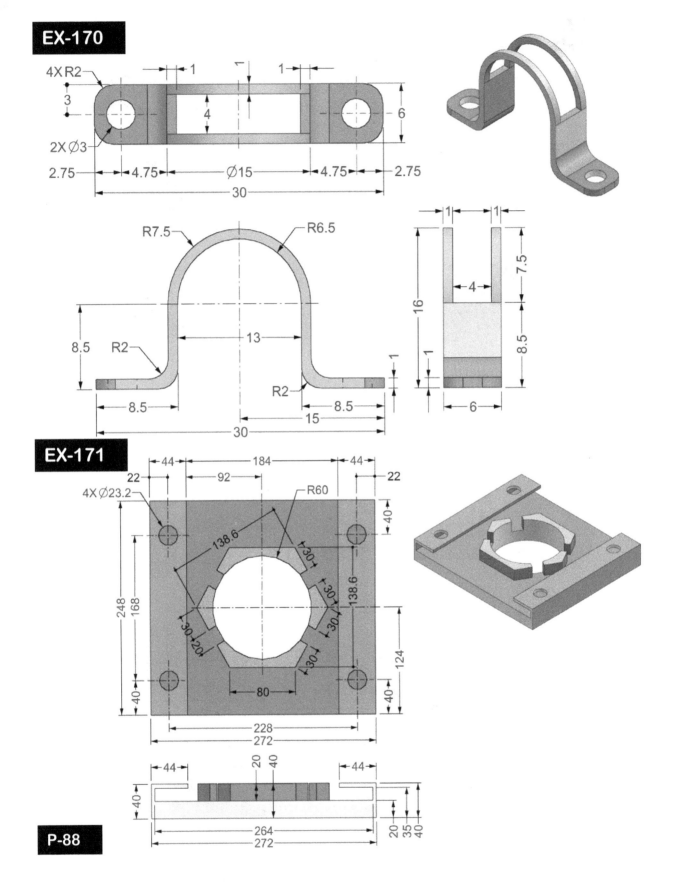

EX-170

4X R2
3
2X Ø3
2.75 4.75 Ø15 4.75 2.75
30
1 1 1
4
6

R7.5 R6.5
R2
8.5
13
R2
8.5 8.5
15
30

1 1
7.5
16
4
1
8.5
6

EX-171

44 184 44
22 92 22
4X Ø23.2
R60
40
138.6
30
30
138.6
248 168
30 30
20 124
80
40
40
228
272

44 20 40 44
40
264 20 35 40
272

P-88

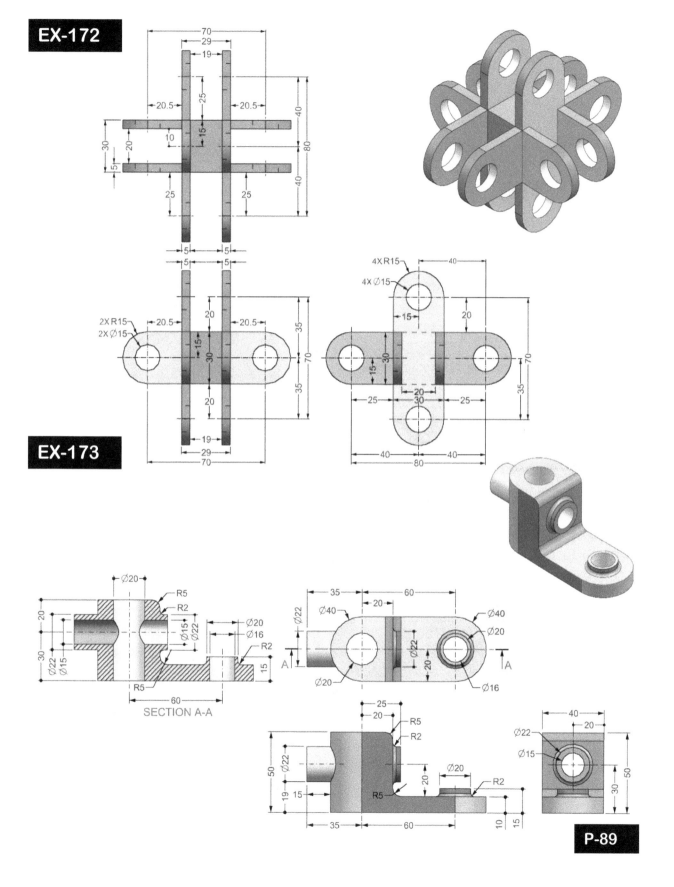

EX-172

EX-173

SECTION A-A

P-89

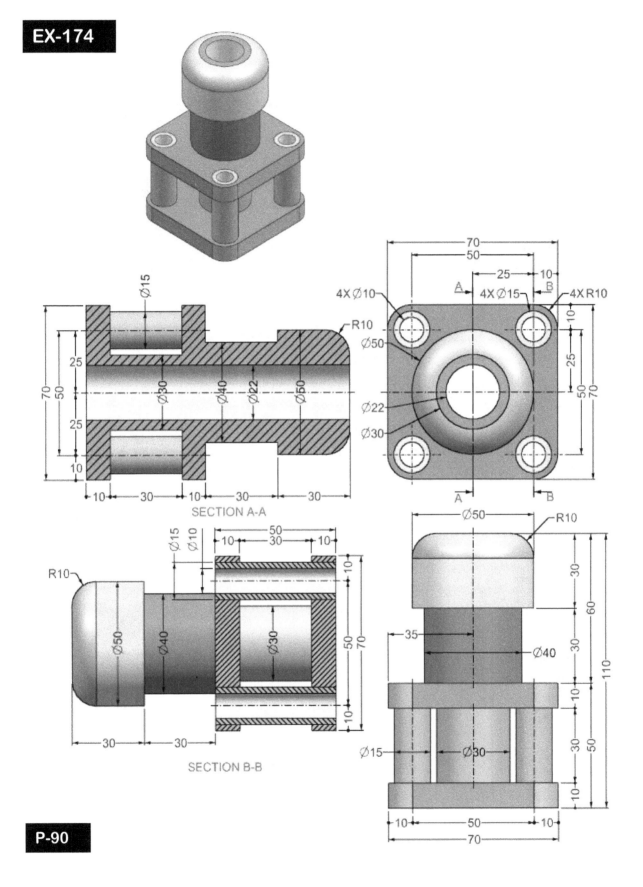

EX-174

SECTION A-A

SECTION B-B

4X Ø10
R10
Ø50
Ø22
Ø30
4X Ø15
4X R10

Ø15
Ø10
R10
Ø50
Ø40
Ø30

Ø50
R10
Ø40
35
Ø15
Ø30

P-90

4X ∅15

4X ∅10

∅30

∅22

70
35
35
10
25
25
10
4X R10

10
35
25
70
25
35
10

A A

∅30
∅15
∅15
∅15
∅15
50
70
20
5
10
30
10
50

∅30
∅22
∅15
∅10
20
30
5
10
70
30
10
∅22
25
25
50
70

SECTION A-A

EX-176

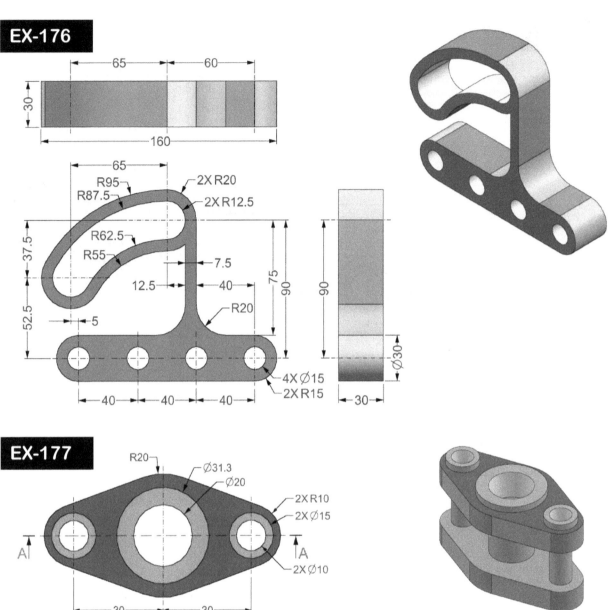

EX-177

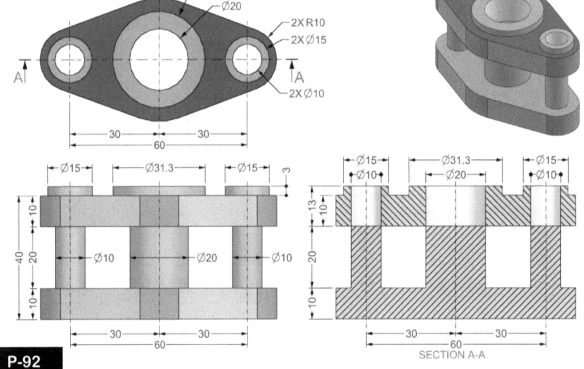

SECTION A-A

P-92

EX-178

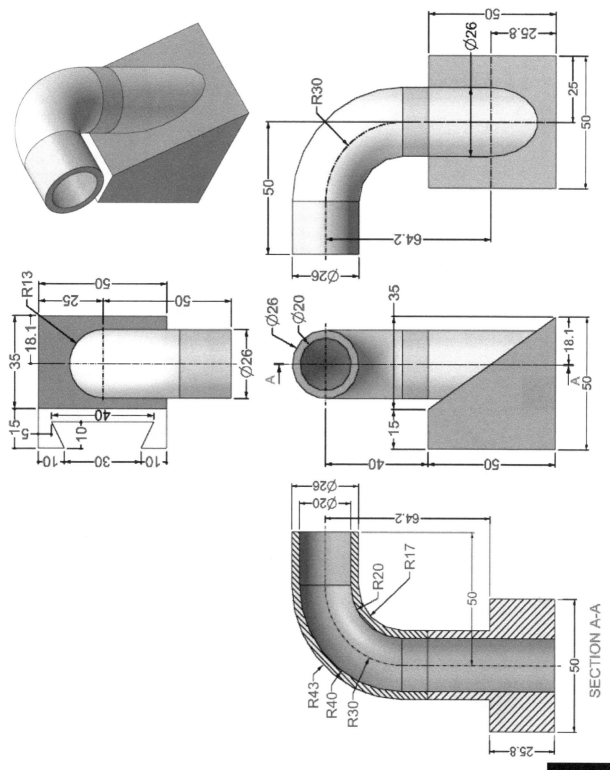

Ø26
Ø20
R17
R20
64.2
50
50
R43
R40
R30
25.8

SECTION A-A

R30
50
Ø26
25.8
Ø26
25
50
64.2

R13
50
25
50
35
18.1
Ø26
15
5
40
10
10
30

Ø26
Ø20
35
18.1
50
15
A
A
40
50

P-93

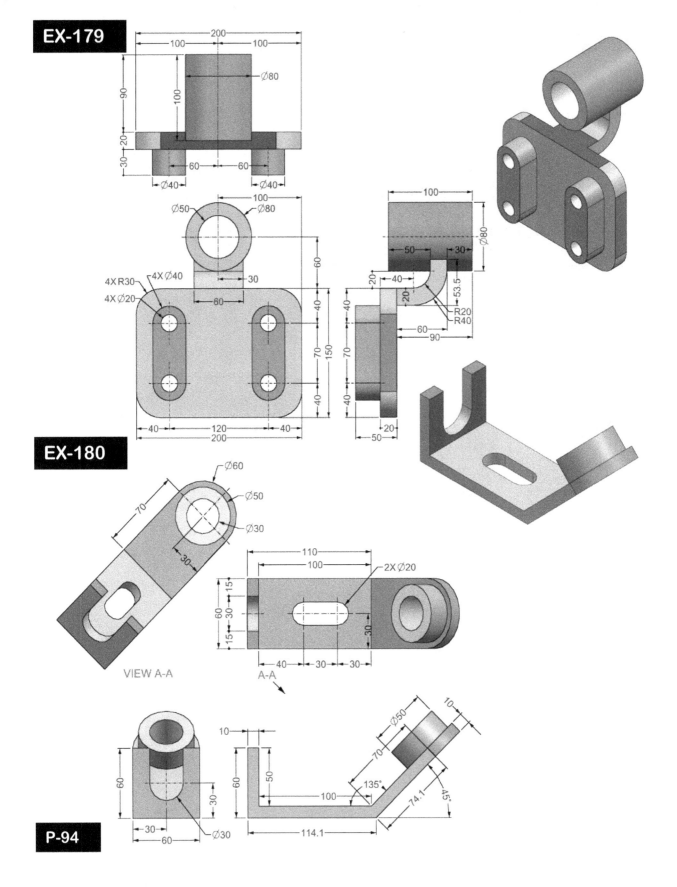

EX-179

200
100
100
Ø80
90
100
20
30
60
60
Ø40
Ø40

Ø50
100
Ø80
60
4X R30
4X Ø40
4X Ø20
30
60
40
70
150
40
40
40
40
120
40
200
20
50

100
50
30
Ø80
20
40
20
53.5
R20
R40
60
90

EX-180

Ø60
Ø50
70
Ø30
30

110
100
2X Ø20
15
15
60
30
30
15
15
40
30
30

VIEW A-A

A-A

P-94

60
30
30
60
Ø30

10
60
50
100
114.1
Ø50
70
10
135°
74.1
45°

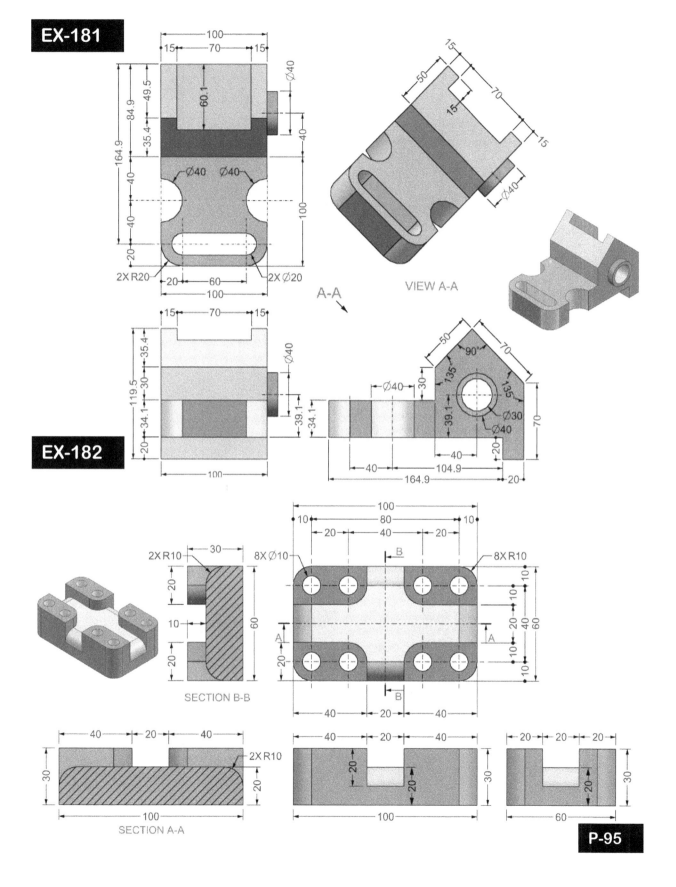

EX-181

Ø40

60.1

Ø40   Ø40

2X R20   2X Ø20

A-A

VIEW A-A

EX-182

Ø40

Ø40

90°

135   135

Ø30
Ø40

SECTION B-B

2X R10

8X Ø10

8X R10

SECTION A-A

2X R10

P-95

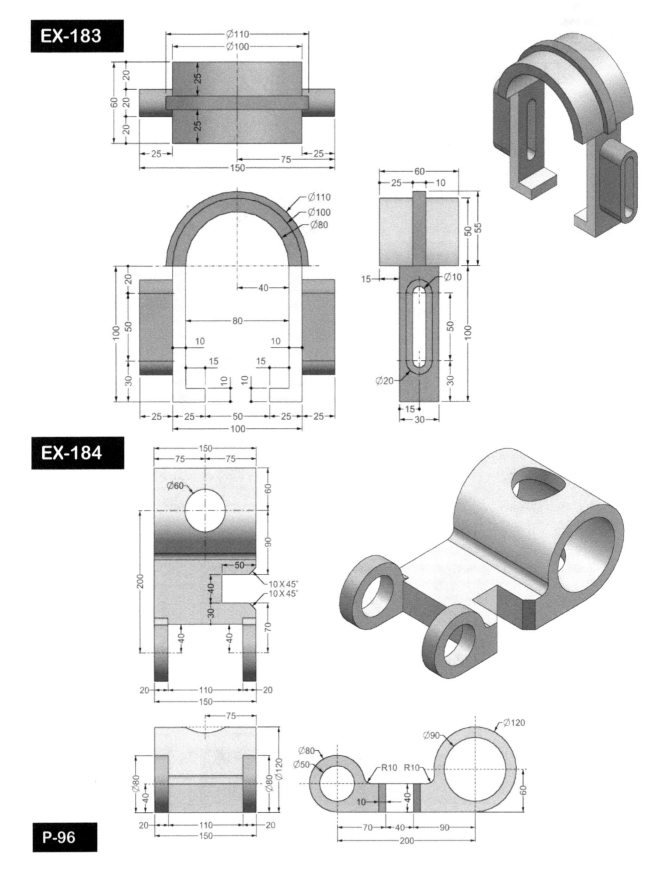

EX-183

EX-184

P-96

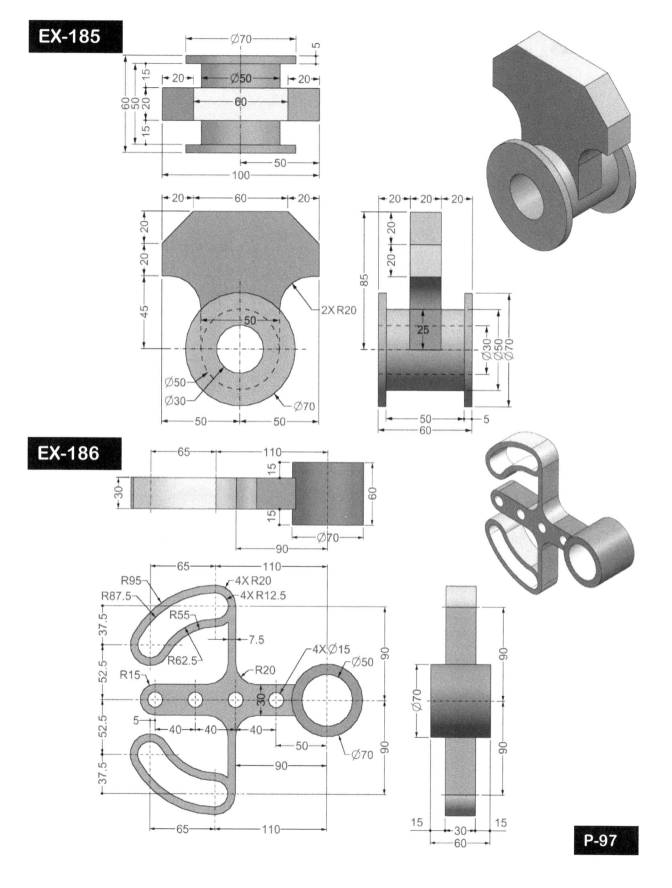

EX-185

EX-186

P-97

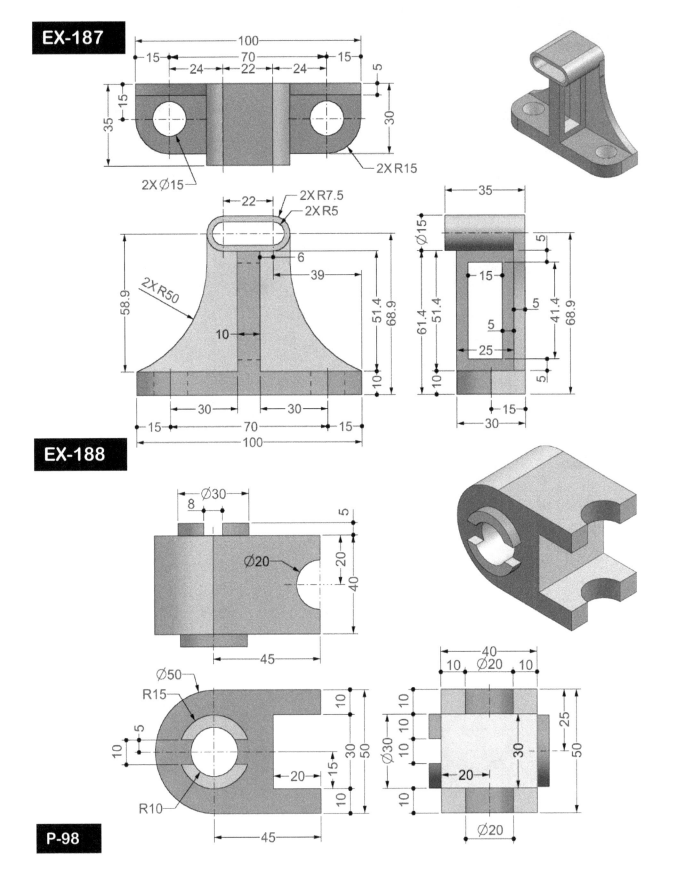

EX-187

100
15 70 15
24 22 24
5
35
15
30
2X R15
2X Ø15

2X R7.5
22 2X R5
6
39
2X R50
58.9
51.4
68.9
10
10
15 70 15
30 30
100

35
Ø15
5
15
61.4
51.4
5
41.4
68.9
5
5
10
25
5
15
30

EX-188

Ø30
8
5
Ø20
20
40
45

Ø50
R15
10
5
10
10
Ø30
10
10
10
30
50
20
15
10
R10
45

40
10 Ø20 10
25
30
50
20
Ø20

P-98

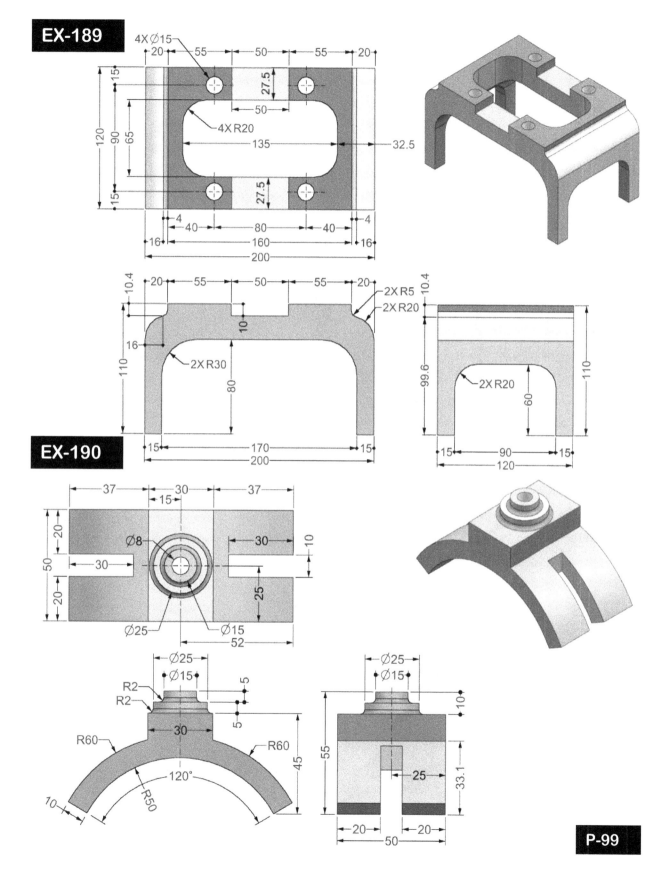

EX-189

4X Ø15
20 — 55 — 50 — 55 — 20
15
120
90
65
27.5
4X R20
135
32.5
15
27.5
4
40 — 80 — 40
4
16 — 160 — 16
200

EX-190

10.4
20 — 55 — 50 — 55 — 20
2X R5
2X R20
10
16
110
2X R30
80
15 — 170 — 15
200

10.4
99.6
110
2X R20
60
15 — 90 — 15
120

37 — 30 — 37
15
50
20
Ø8
30
10
30
20
Ø25
Ø15
25
52

Ø25
Ø15
R2
R2
5
30
5
R60
45
R60
120°
R50
10

Ø25
Ø15
10
55
33.1
25
20 — 20
50

P-99

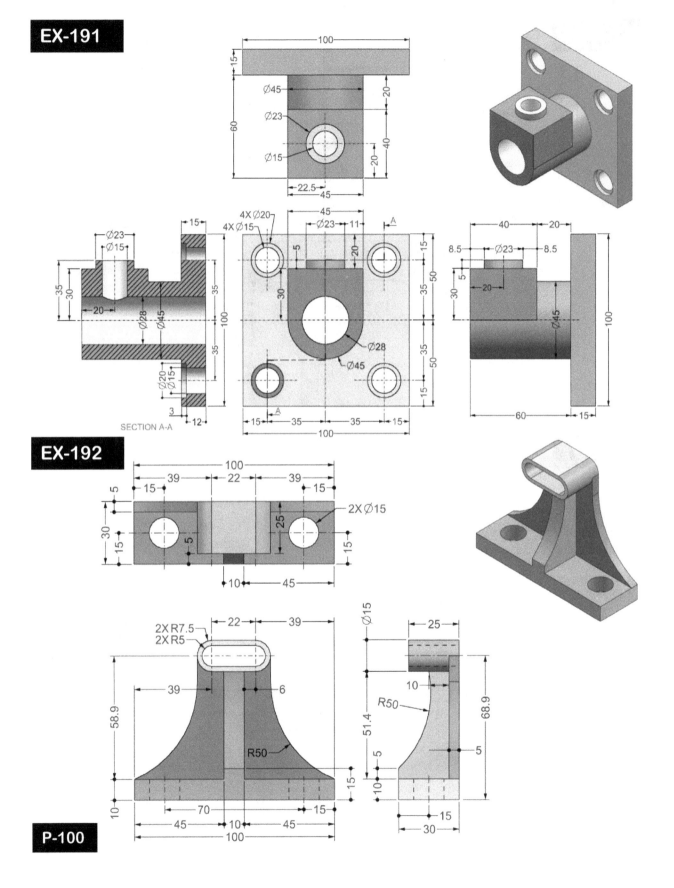

EX-191

EX-192

P-100

SECTION A-A

EX-193

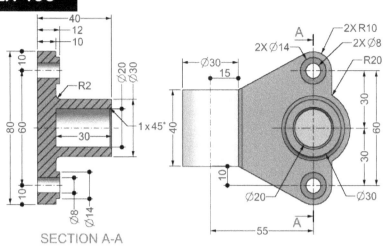

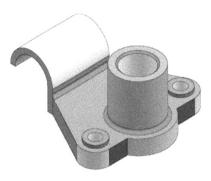

2X R10
2X Ø8
R20
2X Ø14
Ø30
15
40
30
60
30
10
Ø20
Ø30
A
A

40
12
10
R2
Ø20
Ø30
80
60
10
30
1 x 45°
Ø8
Ø14
10
SECTION A-A

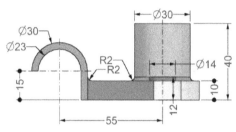

Ø30
Ø23
15
R2
R2
Ø30
Ø14
40
10
12
55

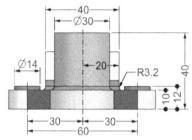

40
Ø30
Ø14
20
R3.2
40
10
12
30
30
60

EX-194

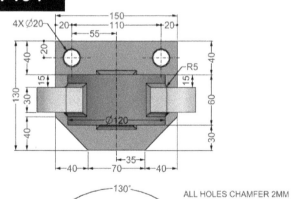

4X Ø20
150
110
20
55
20
40
20
40
R5
130
15
15
30
60
Ø120
40
30
40
70
35
40

ALL HOLES CHAMFER 2MM

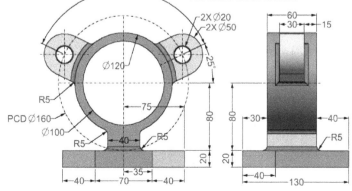

130°
2X Ø20
2X Ø50
Ø120
25°
R5
75
80
PCD Ø160
Ø100
R5
R5
40
20
40
70
35
40

60
30
15
80
30
40
R5
20
40
130

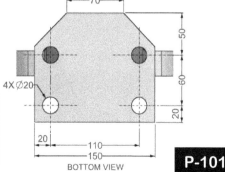

70
50
60
4X Ø20
20
20
110
150
BOTTOM VIEW

P-101

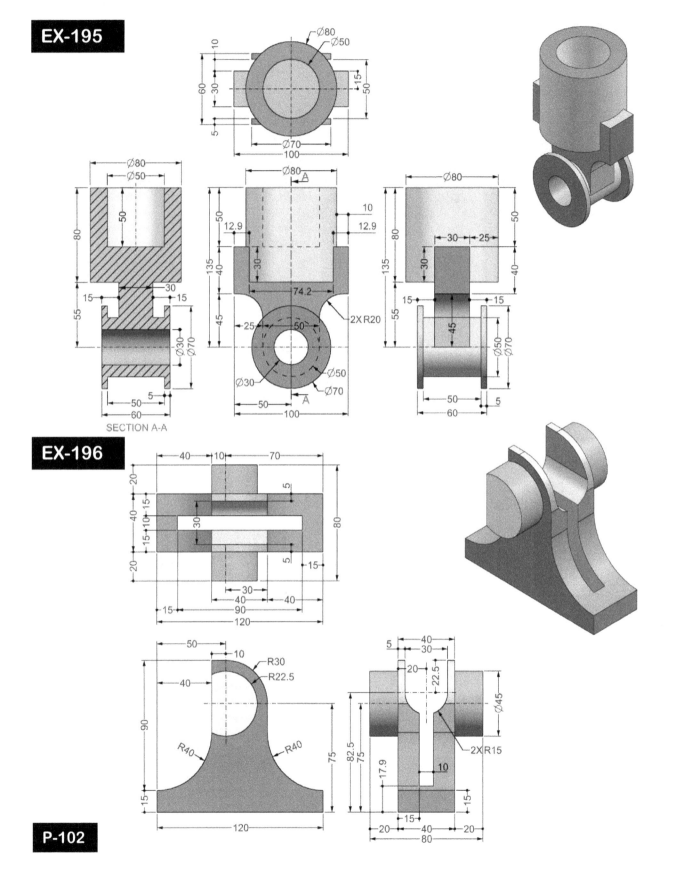

EX-195

Ø80
Ø50
10
60
30
15
50
5
Ø70
100

Ø80
Ø50
50
80
30
15   15
55
Ø30
Ø70
5
50
60
SECTION A-A

Ø80   A
50
10
12.9   12.9
135
40   30
45   74.2
25   50   2X R20
Ø30   Ø50
50   Ø70
100   A

Ø80
50
80
30   25
135   30
15   15
55   45
Ø50
Ø70
50
5
60

EX-196

40   10   70
20
5
40   15
15   10   30   80
15
20   5
15
30
40   40
15
90
120

50   10   R30
40   R22.5
90
R40   R40
75
15
120

5   40
30
20   22.5
82.5   75
17.9   10
15   15
20   40   20
80
2X R15
Ø45

P-102

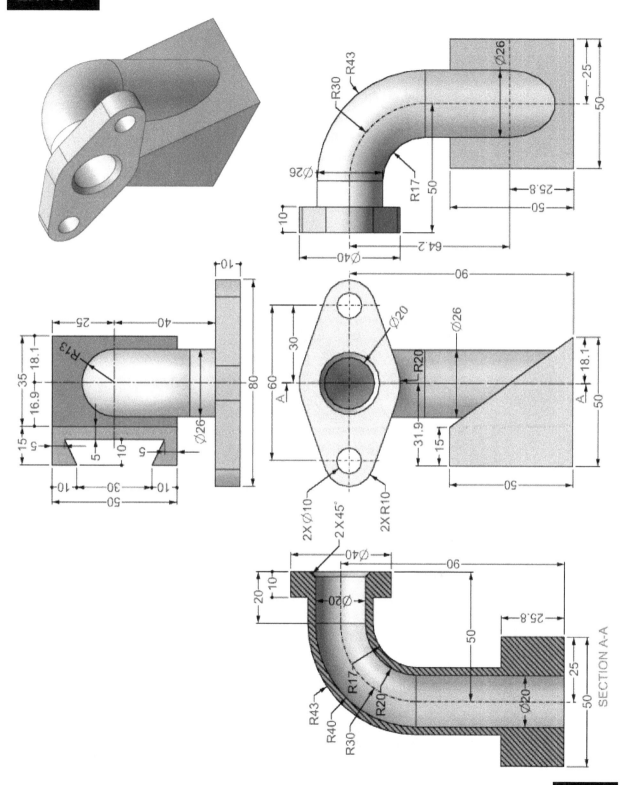

R43
R30
Ø26
Ø26
R17
50
25
50
25.8
50
10
64.2
Ø40

10
25
40
R13
35
18.1
16.9
15
5
5
10
5
Ø26
80
10
30
10
50

30
60
A
Ø20
R20
Ø26
A
18.1
31.9
15
50
50
90

2X Ø10
2 X 45°
2XR10

Ø40
Ø20
90
20
10
R17
R20
50
R43
R40
R30
25.8
25
Ø20
50

SECTION A-A

6X Ø15 THRU
ON PCD 90

Ø120

Ø50

Ø40

PCD Ø90

A

A

Ø120

Ø50

Ø40

15

10

Ø15

120

30

60°

60°

80

5

10

Ø20

Ø30

PCD 54

Ø10

SECTION A-A

B-B

VIEW B-B

8X Ø10 THRU
ON PCD 54

Ø20

Ø30

Ø70

PCD Ø54

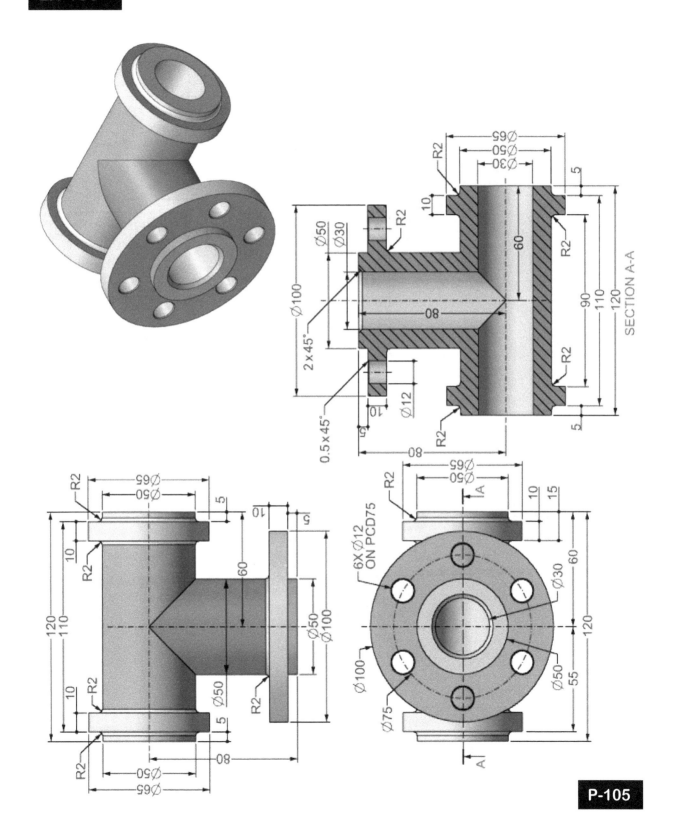

SECTION A-A

P-105

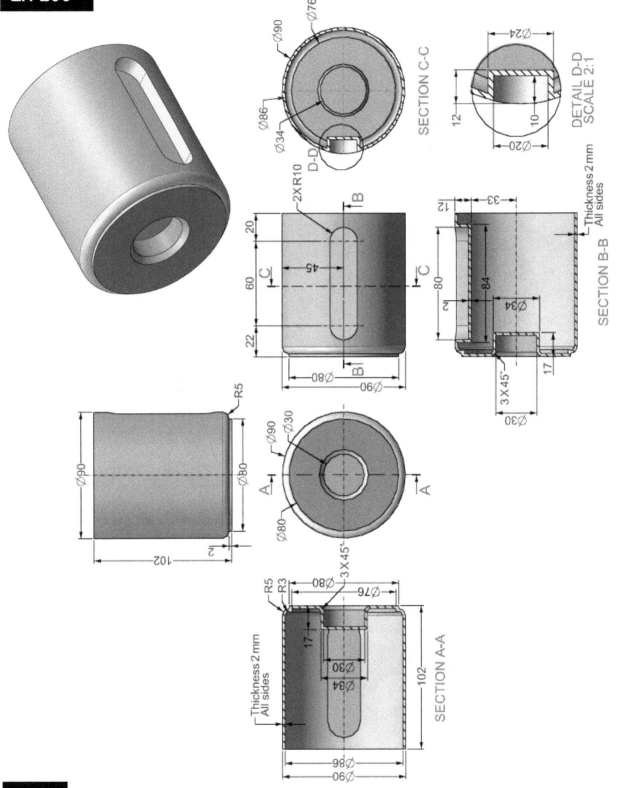

Ø76
Ø90
Ø86
Ø34
D-D
SECTION C-C

Ø24
12
10
Ø20
DETAIL D-D
SCALE 2:1

2×R10
20
C
45
60
22
B
B
Ø80
Ø90

12
33
Thickness 2 mm
All sides
80
84
Ø34
12
3 X 45°
17
Ø30
SECTION B-B

R5
Ø90
Ø80
2
102

Ø90
Ø30
A
A
Ø80
3 X 45°

R5
R3
Ø80
Ø76
3 X 45°
17
Ø30
Ø84
102
98Ø
Ø90
Thickness 2 mm
All sides
SECTION A-A

Other useful books by CADIN360

1. 150 CAD Exercises

2. AutoCAD Exercises

3. CAD Exercises

4. 50+ SolidWorks Exercises

5. SolidWorks 200 Exercises

6. Autodesk Inventor Exercises

7. Catia Exercises

8. Siemens NX Exercises